Scale 1:250,000 or 3.95 miles to 1 inch (2.5km to 1cm)

Some islands are shown at smaller sca...

Motoring information

Motorway with number	Restricted primary route junctions	Narrow primary/other A/B road with passing places (Scotland)	Railway line, in tunnel	Park and Ride (at least 6 days per week)
Toll motorway with toll station	Primary route service area	Road under construction	Railway station, tram stop, level crossing	City, town, village or other built-up area
Motorway junction with and without number	Primary route destination	Road tunnel	Preserved or tourist railway	Height in metres
Restricted motorway junctions	Other A road single/ dual carriageway	Road toll, steep gradient (arrows point downhill)	Airport (major/minor)	Mountain pass
Motorway service area, rest area	B road single/ dual carriageway	Distance in miles between symbols	Heliport	Snow gates (on main routes)
Motorway and junction under construction	Minor road more than 4 metres wide, less than 4 metres wide	Vehicle ferry (all year, seasonal)	International freight terminal	National boundary
Primary route single/ dual carriageway	Roundabout	Fast vehicle ferry or catamaran	24-hour Accident & Emergency hospital	County or administrative boundary
Primary route junction with and without number	Interchange/junction	Passenger ferry (all year, seasonal)	Crematorium	City with clean air zone, low/zero emission zone

Touring information

To avoid disappointment, check opening times before visiting

Scenic route	Industrial interest	RSPB site	Cave or cavern	National Trust site
Tourist Information Centre	Aqueduct, viaduct	National Nature Reserve (England, Scotland, Wales)	Windmill, monument or memorial	National Trust for Scotland site
Tourist Information Centre (seasonal)	Vineyard	Local nature reserve	Beach (award winning)	English Heritage site
Visitor or heritage centre	Brewery or distillery	Wildlife Trust reserve	Lighthouse	Historic Scotland site
Picnic site	Garden	Forest drive	Golf course	Cadw (Welsh heritage) site
Caravan site (AA inspected)	Arboretum	National trail	Football stadium	Other place of interest
Camping site (AA inspected)	Country park	Viewpoint	County cricket ground	Boxed symbols indicate attractions within urban area
Caravan & camping site (AA inspected)	Showground	Waterfall	Rugby Union national stadium	World Heritage Site (UNESCO)
Abbey, cathedral or priory	Theme park	Hill-fort	International athletics stadium	National Park and National Scenic Area (Scotland)
Ruined abbey, cathedral or priory	Farm or animal centre	Roman antiquity	Horse racing, show jumping	Forest Park
Castle	Zoological or wildlife collection	Prehistoric monument	Motor-racing circuit	Sandy beach
Historic house or building	Bird collection	Battle site with year	Air show venue	Heritage coast
Museum or art gallery	Aquarium	Preserved or tourist railway	Ski slope (natural, artificial)	Major shopping centre

43rd edition June 2024 © AA Media Limited 2024
Revised version of the atlas formerly known as *AA Big Road Atlas*. Original edition printed 1981.

All cartography in this atlas edited, designed and produced by the Mapping Services Department of AA Media Limited (A05873).

This atlas contains Ordnance Survey data © Crown copyright and database right 2024. Contains public sector information licensed under the Open Government Licence v3.0. Ireland mapping contains data available from openstreetmap.org © under the Open Database License found at opendatacommons.org

Published by AA Media Limited, whose registered office is Grove House, Lutyens Close, Basingstoke, Hampshire RG24 8AG, UK. Registered number 06112600. All rights reserved. No part of this publication may be reproduced, stored in a retrieval system, or transmitted in any form or by any means – electronic, mechanical, photocopying, recording or otherwise – unless the permission of the publisher has been given beforehand.

A CIP catalogue record for this book is available from The British Library.

* Nielsen BookScan Total Consumer Market (UK Standard scale atlases) 1–52 weeks to 1 January 2024.

Disclaimer: The contents of this atlas are believed to be correct at the time of the latest revision, it will not contain any subsequent amended, new or temporary information including diversions and traffic control or enforcement systems. The publishers cannot be held responsible or liable for any loss or damage occasioned to any person acting or refraining from action as a result of any use or reliance on material in this atlas, nor for any errors, omissions or changes in such material. This does not affect your statutory rights.

The publishers would welcome information to correct any errors or omissions and to keep this atlas up to date. Please write to the Atlas Editor, AA Media Limited, Grove House, Lutyens Close, Basingstoke, Hampshire RG24 8AG, UK. **E-mail:** *roadatlasfeedback@aamediagroup.co.uk*

Acknowledgements: AA Media Limited would like to thank the following for information used in the creation of this atlas: Cadw, English Heritage, Forestry Commission, Historic Scotland, National Trust and National Trust for Scotland, RSPB, The Wildlife Trust, Scottish Natural Heritage, Natural England, The Countryside Council for Wales. Award winning beaches from 'Blue Flag' and 'Keep Scotland Beautiful' (summer 2023 data): for latest information visit *www.blueflag.org* and *www.keepscotlandbeautiful.org.* Ireland mapping: Republic of Ireland census 2016 © Central Statistics Office and Northern Ireland census 2016 © NISRA (population data); Irish Public Sector Data (CC BY 4.0) (Gaeltacht); Logainm.ie (placenames); Roads Service and Transport Infrastructure Ireland
Printed by Walstead Peterborough, UK

Map pages & route planner

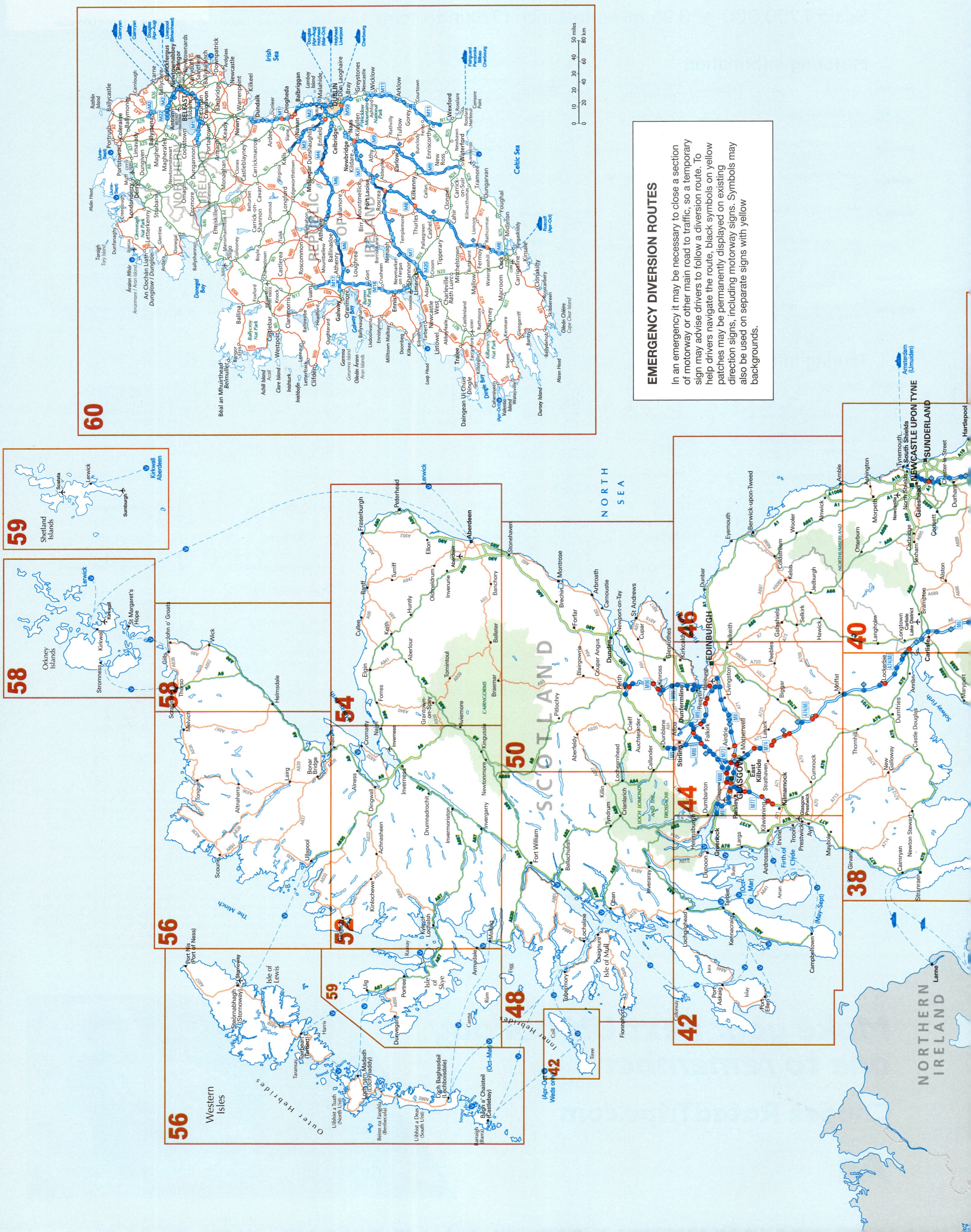

EMERGENCY DIVERSION ROUTES

In an emergency it may be necessary to close a section of motorway or other main road to traffic, so a temporary sign may advise drivers to follow a diversion route. To help drivers navigate the route, black symbols on yellow patches may be permanently displayed on existing direction signs, including motorway signs. Symbols may also be used on separate signs with yellow backgrounds.

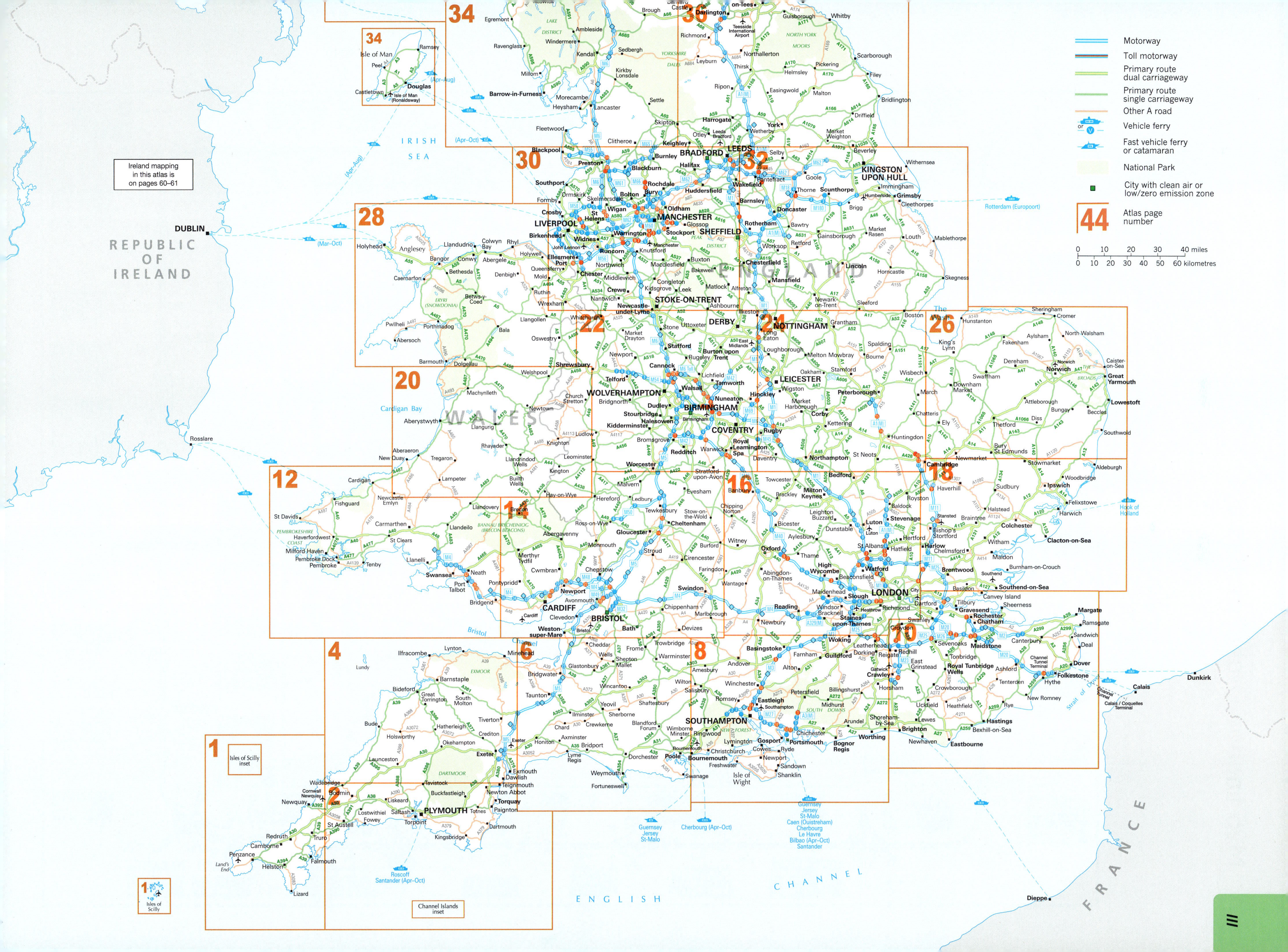

Motorway
Toll motorway
Primary route dual carriageway
Primary route single carriageway
Other A road
Vehicle ferry
Fast vehicle ferry or catamaran
National Park
City with clean air or low/zero emission zone
44 Atlas page number
0 10 20 30 40 miles
0 10 20 30 40 50 60 kilometres
Ireland mapping in this atlas is on pages 60–61
REPUBLIC OF IRELAND
DUBLIN
IRISH SEA
WALES
ENGLAND
ENGLISH CHANNEL
FRANCE
Isles of Scilly inset
Channel Islands inset
LONDON
BIRMINGHAM
MANCHESTER
LIVERPOOL
LEEDS
BRADFORD
SHEFFIELD
NOTTINGHAM
LEICESTER
COVENTRY
WOLVERHAMPTON
STOKE-ON-TRENT
DERBY
CARDIFF
BRISTOL
SOUTHAMPTON
PLYMOUTH
KINGSTON UPON HULL

M25 London Orbital motorway

Refer also to atlas pages 9–10 and 17–18

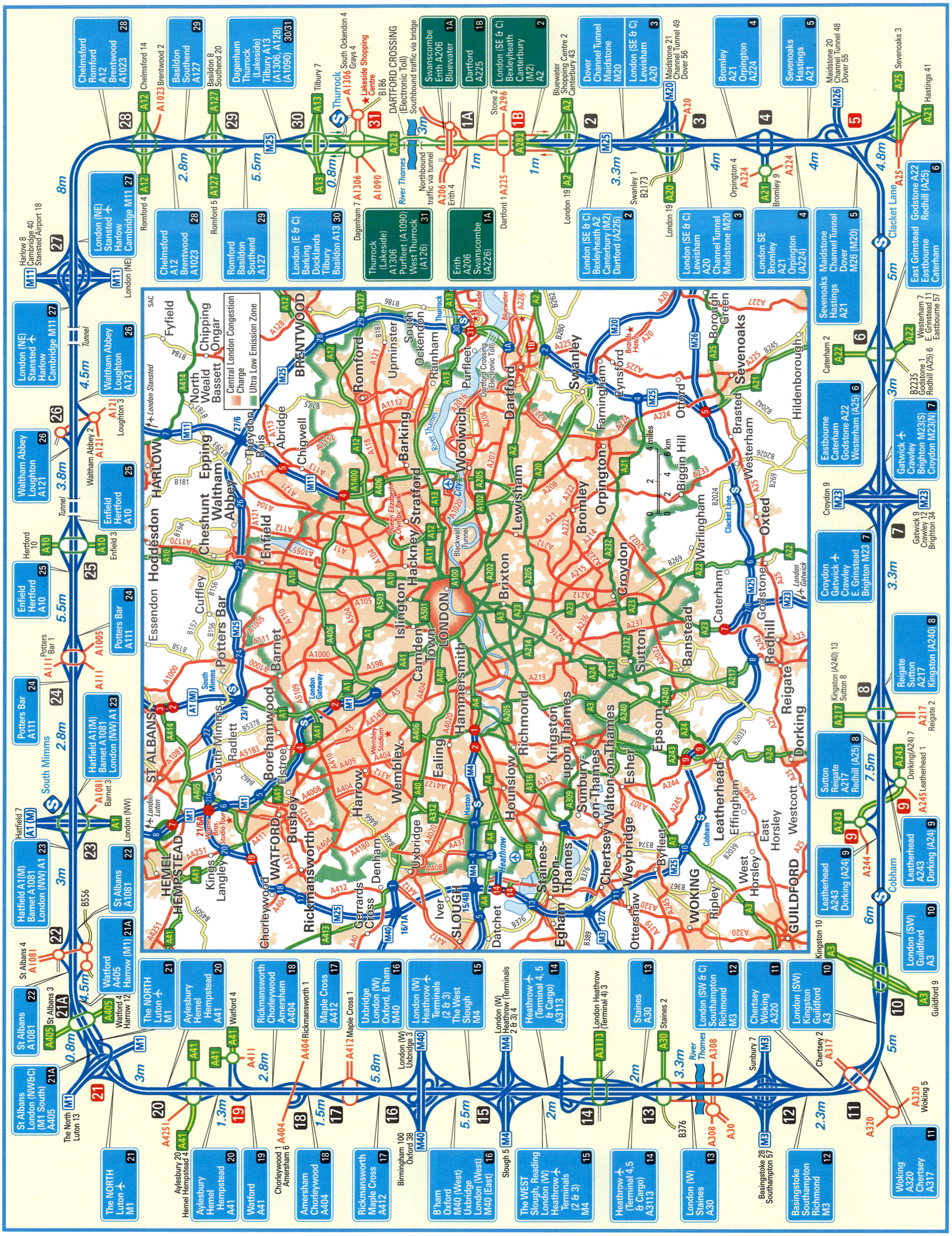

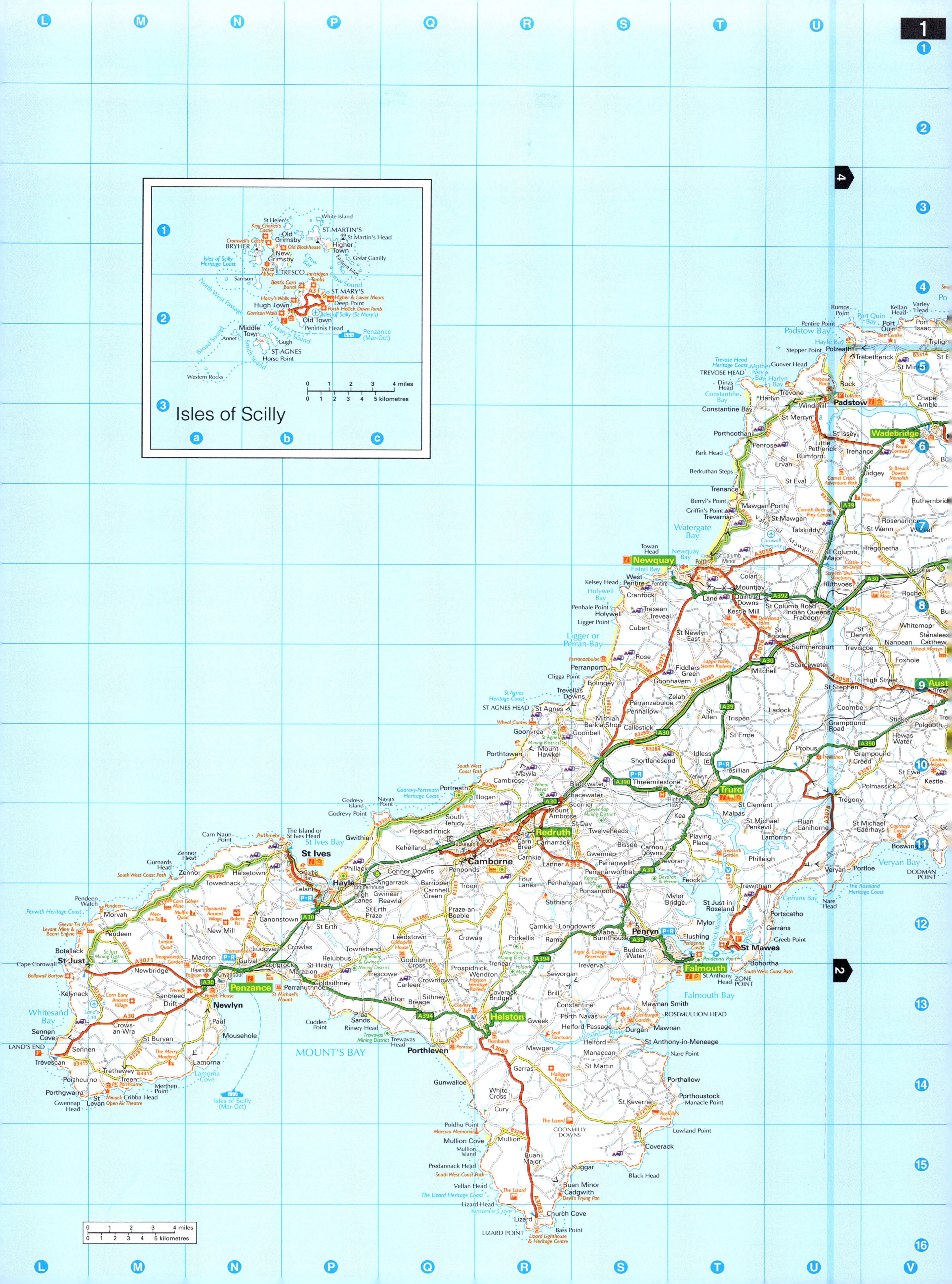
L
M
N
P
Q
R
S
T
U
V
1
2
3
4
5
6
7
8
9
10
11
12
13
14
15
16
Isles of Scilly
St Helen's
King Charles's Castle
White Island
ST MARTIN'S
St Martin's Head
Old Grimsby
Cromwell's Castle
BRYHER
Old Blockhouse
Higher Town
New Grimsby
Isles of Scilly Heritage Coast
Great Ganilly
Tresco Abbey
TRESCO
Innisidgen Tombs
Samson
Bant's Carn Burial
Crow Sound
ST MARY'S
North West Passage
Harry's Walls
Higher & Lower Moors
Hugh Town
Deep Point
Garrison Walls
Porth Hellick Down Tomb
Old Town
Isles of Scilly (St Mary's)
Peninnis Head
Middle Town
Penzance (Mar-Oct)
Annet
St Mary's Sound
Broad Sound
Gugh
ST AGNES
Horse Point
Smith Sound
Western Rocks
4 miles
5 kilometres
Padstow Bay
Pentire Point
Rumps Point
Port Quin Bay
Port Quin
Kellan Head
Varley Head
Port Isaac
Hayle Bay
Polzeath
Stepper Point
Trebetherick
Trevose Head Heritage Coast
Mother Ivey's Bay
Gunver Head
TREVOSE HEAD
Harlyn Bay
Dinas Head
Constantine Bay
Trevone
Harlyn
Rock
Padstow
Windmill
St Merryn
Chapel Amble
Porthcothan
St Issey
Wadebridge
Little Petherick
Penrose
Trenance
Park Head
St Ervan
Rumford
St Jidgey
Bedruthan Steps
St Eval
Trenance
Berryl's Point
Griffin's Point
Mawgan Porth
Trevarrian
St Mawgan
Rosenannon
Watergate Bay
Vale of Mawgan
Talskiddy
St Wenn
Towan Head
Newquay
Newquay Bay
St Columb Minor
St Columb Major
Tregonetha
Fistral Bay
Porth
Victoria
Kelsey Head
West Pentire
Colan
Holywell Bay
Crantock
Mountjoy
Ruthvoes
Penhale Point
Quintrell Downs
Roche
Holywell
Trevemper
Lane
Tresean
Treveal
Kestle Mill
St Columb Road
Indian Queens
Fraddon
Ligger Point
Cubert
St Newlyn East
St Enoder
Whitemoor
Ligger or Perran Bay
Summercourt
St Dennis
Nanpean
Treviscoe
Stenalees
Carthew
Perranporth
Rose
Mitchell
Foxhole
Fiddlers Green
Cligga Point
Bolingey
Goonhavern
Scarcewater
High Street
St Agnes Heritage Coast
Trevellas
Zelah
St Stephen
ST AGNES HEAD
St Agnes
Perranzabuloe
Penhallow
St Allen
Trispen
Ladock
Coombe
Mithian
Barkla Shop
Callestick
Grampound Road
Sticker
Goonvrea
Goonbell
St Erme
Hewas Water
Polgooth
Mount Hawke
Probus
Grampound
Porthtowan
Shortlanesend
Idless
Creed
St Ewe
Kestle
Mawla
Tresillian
Blackwater
Threemilestone
South West Coast Path
Portreath
Illogan
Cambrose
Truro
Polmassick
Godrevy Island
Navax Point
Godrevy-Portreath Heritage Coast
Chacewater
Tregony
St Clement
Godrevy Point
South Tehidy
Scorrier
Malpas
Mount Ambrose
St Day
Twelveheads
Kea
St Michael Penkevil
Ruan Lanihorne
St Michael Caerhays
Reskadinnick
Redruth
Gwithian
The Island or St Ives Head
Carn Naun Point
St Ives Bay
Carharrack
Playing Place
Lamorran
Boswinger
St Ives
Kehelland
Carn Brea
Bissoe
Carnon Downs
Philleigh
Zennor Head
Camborne
Carnkie
Gwennap
Perranwell
Devoran
Veryan Bay
Gurnards Head
Lanner
DODMAN POINT
Zennor
Halsetown
Connor Downs
Pengegon
Perranarwothal
Veryan
Portloe
Phillack
Towednack
Lelant
Hayle
Angarrack
Barripper
Penponds
Four Lanes
Penhalvean
Ponsanooth
Feock
Trewithian
Carnhell Green
Troon
The Roseland Heritage Coast
Pendeen Watch
Copperhouse
High Lanes
Gwinear
Reawla
Mylor Bridge
Nare Head
Penwith Heritage Coast
Morvah
Stithians
St Erth Praze
Praze-an-Beeble
St Just-in-Roseland
Portscatho
Canonstown
Gerrans Bay
Pendeen
New Mill
St Erth
Carnkie
Longdowns
Mylor
Gerrans
Crowlas
Leedstown
Crowan
Porkellis
Rame
Mabe Burnthouse
Penryn
Flushing
Greeb Point
Botallack
Ludgvan
Townshend
St Mawes
Cape Cornwall
St Just
Madron
Gulval
Relubbus
Godolphin Cross
Prospidnick
Trenear
Budock Water
Bohortha
Newbridge
Heamoor
Longrock
St Hilary
Wendron
Treverva
Falmouth
St Anthony Head
ZONE POINT
Marazion
Trescowe
Crowntown
Seworgan
Kelynack
Penzance
Perranuthnoe
Goldsithney
Carleen
Coverack Bridges
Brill
Falmouth Bay
Sancreed
Newlyn
Ashton
Sithney
Breage
Helston
Constantine
Mawnan Smith
Whitesand Bay
Drift
Gweek
Porth Navas
ROSEMULLION HEAD
Paul
Cudden Point
Praa Sands
Rinsey Head
Helford Passage
Durgan
Mawnan
Sennen Cove
Crows-an-Wra
Mousehole
Trewavas Head
Helford
St Anthony-in-Meneage
LAND'S END
St Buryan
MOUNT'S BAY
Porthleven
Mawgan
Manaccan
Nare Point
Sennen
Trevescan
Lamorna
Lamorna Cove
St Martin
Trethewey
Garras
Treen
Porthcurno
Merthen Point
Porthallow
Porthgwarra
Cribba Head
Gunwalloe
Porthoustock
Manacle Point
Gwennap Head
St Levan
Minack Open Air Theatre
Isles of Scilly (Mar-Oct)
White Cross
St Keverne
Cury
GOONHILLY DOWNS
Lowland Point
Poldhu Point
Marconi Memorial
Mullion Cove
Mullion
Coverack
Mullion Island
Ruan Major
Predannack Head
Kuggar
Black Head
Vellan Head
Ruan Minor
Cadgwith
The Lizard Heritage Coast
Lizard Head
Kynance Cove
Church Cove
Lizard
LIZARD POINT
Bass Point
Lizard Lighthouse & Heritage Centre
A30
A39
A390
A392
A394
A393
A3075
A3058
A3059
A3071
A3083
A3078
A31
B3306
B3315
B3283
B3296
B3293
B3294
B3284
B3285
B3300
B3301
B3280
B3297
B3314
4 miles
5 kilometres

BODMIN MOOR
Tintagel
TINTAGEL HEAD
Boscastle
Trevalga
Camelford
Port Isaac
Port Isaac Bay
Padstow Bay
Padstow
Polzeath
Wadebridge
Bodmin
Launceston
Tavistock
Callington
Liskeard
Lostwithiel
St Austell
Fowey
Looe
Looe Bay
Polperro
Saltash
Torpoint
PLYMOUTH
Plymouth Sound
Whitsand Bay
RAME HEAD
Mevagissey
Mevagissey Bay
St Austell Bay
GRIBBIN HEAD
DODMAN POINT
Veryan Bay
Gerrans Bay
St Mawes
Truro
St Columb Major
St Columb Road
Indian Queens
Fraddon
Roche
Lanivet
Lanhydrock
West Taphouse
East Taphouse
Lanreath
Pelynt
Menheniot
St Germans
Kingsand
Cawsand
Cremyll
Millbrook
Gunnislake
Calstock
Altarnun
Fivelanes
North Hill
Minions
Upton
St Cleer
St Neot
Warleggan
Blisland
St Breward
St Teath
Delabole
Davidstow
Otterham
Marshgate
Lifton
Milton Abbot
Bere Alston
Bere Ferrers
Tamerton Foliot
Pentewan
Polgooth
Grampound
Probus
Tregony
Portscatho
Gerrans
Portloe
Veryan
Ruan Lanihorne
St Just-in-Roseland
Polruan
Lansallos
Herodsfoot
St Keyne
Duloe
Sandplace
Widegates
Hessenford
Downderry
Seaton
Portwrinkle
Crafthole
Antony
Sheviock
Landrake
Botusfleming
Landulph
Cargreen
Stoke Climsland
Kelly Bray
Pensilva
Common Moor
Darite
Tremar
Merrymeet
Quethiock
Pillaton
St Mellion
Harrowbarrow
Metherell
St Dominick
Albaston
Latchley
Chilsworthy
Gulworthy
Lamerton
Peter Tavy
Mary Tavy
Horrabridge
Yelverton
Buckland Monachorum
Milton Combe
Roborough
Crownhill
Roscoff
Santander (Apr-Oct)
Guernsey
St Peter Port
St Sampson
Vale
L'Ancresse
L'Ancresse Bay
Grandes Rocques
Cobo
Cobo Bay
Vazon Bay
Castel
King's Mills
Le Villocq
St Saviour
St Andrew
St Martin
St Peter's
Forest
Torteval
Pleinmont Point
Rocquaine Bay
L'Eree
Perelle Bay
Saints Bay
Icart Point
Jerbourg
Havelet Bay
Village de Putron
Bordeaux
Les Quartiers
Channel Islands
ALDERNEY
St Anne
HERM
SARK
JERSEY
St Helier
FRANCE
Alderney
Herm
Sark
Jersey
Portsmouth
Poole
Diélette
St Malo
Grande Havre
Saline Bay
Petit Bot Bay
Moulin Huet Bay

DARTMOOR
DARTMOOR FOREST
DARTMOOR NATIONAL PARK
Exeter
Topsham
Exmouth
Budleigh Salterton
Sidmouth
Seaton
Beer
Dawlish
Teignmouth
Bovey Tracey
Kingsteignton
Newton Abbot
Kingskerswell
Ashburton
Buckfastleigh
Babbacombe Bay
TORQUAY
Paignton
Tor Bay
Brixham
BERRY HEAD
Totnes
Dartmouth
Ivybridge
Plympton
Kingsbridge
Salcombe
Bigbury Bay
Start Bay
Start Point
Bolt Head
Prawle Point
Princetown
Chagford
Moretonhampstead
Dunsford
Chudleigh
Lympstone
Starcross
Dawlish Warren
Harford
Cornwood
Modbury
Yealmpton
Slapton
Torcross
Beesands
Chillington
Stokenham
Frogmore
Thurlestone
Hope
East Prawle
Kingswear
Stoke Fleming
Strete
Blackpool
Jersey
0 1 2 miles
0 1 2 kilometres
St Ouen's Bay
St Ouen
St Mary
St John
Trinity
St Martin
Gorey
Royal Bay of Grouville
Grouville
St Clement
St Helier
St Aubin
St Aubin's Bay
St Brelade
St Brelade's Bay
St Peter
St Lawrence
St Saviour
Corbière Point
La Rocque
Bouley Bay
Rozel Bay
Plémont Point
Grosnez Point
Sorel Point
Ronez Point
Noirmont Point
Guernsey, Poole
Guernsey, Portsmouth
Sark
St-Malo
Granville (Apr-Sept)
Barneville-Carteret (Apr-Sept)
a
b
c
d
e
L
M
N
P
Q
R
S
T
U
V
1
2
3
4
5
6
7
8
9
10
11
12
13
14
15
16

B
C
D
E
F
G
H
J
K
1
2
3
4
5
6
7
8
9
10
11
12
13
14
15
16
North West Point
LUNDY
Lundy Heritage Coast
Marine Reserve
Shutter Point
Surf Point
(Apr-Oct)
Ilfracombe
Lee
Slade
Bull Point
Rockham Bay
Mortehoe
Morte Point
Woolacombe
Morte Bay
Trimstone
North Buckland
Baggy Point
Georgeham
Croyde
Croyde Bay
Darracott
Knowle
Saunton
Braunton
North Devon Heritage Coast
Braunton Burrows
Wrafton
Heanton Punchardon
Chivenor
River Taw
Fremington
BARNSTAPLE
OR
BIDEFORD BAY
Crow Point
Appledore
Northam
Westward Ho!
Instow
Westleigh
Eastleigh
Horwood
HARTLAND POINT
Shipload Bay
Titchberry
Damehole Point
Hartland Abbey & Gardens
Stoke
Hartland
Hartland Quay
Speke's Mill Mouth
Milford
Philham
Clovelly
Buck's Mills
Buck's Cross
Horns Cross
Fairy Cross
Ford
Abbotsham
Bideford
Hartland Heritage Coast
Woodtown
Alverdiscott
Landcross
Littleham
Saltrens
Goldworthy
Parkham
Woolfardisworthy
Hardisworthy
Buckland Brewer
Monkleigh
Frithelstock
Frithelstock Stone
Weare Giffard
Huntshaw
Great Torrington
Little Torrington
Welcombe
Darracott
Meddon
Ashmansworthy
East Putford
West Putford
Gooseham
Dinworthy
Haytown
Langtree
Morwenstow
Higher Sharpnose Point
South West Coast Path
Shop
Woodford
Bradworthy
Bulkworthy
Stibb Cross
Peters Marland
Winswell
Lower Sharpnose Point
Steeple Point
Kilkhampton
Stibb
Tamar Lakes
Sutcombe
Sutcombemill
Abbots Bickington
Newton St Petrock
Venngreen
Milton Damerel
Sandy Mouth
Northcott Mouth
Crooklets
Summerleaze
Poughill
Flexbury
Stratton
Bude
Bude Bay
Dunsdon
Holsworthy Beacon
Thornbury
Shebbear
North Town
Petrockstowe
Buckland Filleigh
Woodacott
Bradford
Grimscott
Chilsworthy
Cookbury
Sheepwash
Pancrasweek
Holemoor
Black Torrington
Holsworthy
Hollacombe
Highampton
Marhamchurch
Widemouth Bay
Titson
Bridgerule
Pyworthy
Chasty
Halwill Junction
Halwill
Beaworthy
Dizzard Point
Poundstock
Bangors
Clawton
Treskinnick Cross
Whitstone
Week St Mary
St Gennys
Crackington Haven
Cambeak
Coxford
North Tamerton
Tetcott
Jacobstow
Southcott
Ashwater
Higher Prestacott
Sweets
Wainhouse Corner
Maxworthy
Chapmans Well
Virginstow
Germansweek
Marshgate
Canworthy Water
Otterham
Boyton
Northcott
Bratton Clovelly
Tresparrett
Boscastle
Trevalga
Pentire Point - Widemouth Heritage Coast
Warbstow
Lesnewth
North Petherwin
St Giles-on-the-Heath
Broadwoodwidger
Bridestowe
TINTAGEL HEAD
Tintagel
Trethevey
Bossiney
Treneglos
Tremaine
Petherwin Gate
Hellescott
Yeolmbridge
Old Post Office
Penhallic Point
Treknow
Davidstow
Tremail
Tresmeer
Tregeare
Egloskerry
Langore
Werrington
Stowford
Lewdown
Lobhillcross
Trewarmett
Vale of Avalon
Laneast
Newport
Launceston
Liftondown
Tinhay
Lewtrenchard
Portgate
Lydford
Lifton
Dippertown
Camelford
St Clether
Tregadillett
Trewen
Crowdy Reservoir
South West Coast Path
Delabole
Pengelly
Port Isaac Bay
Westdowns
Lanteglos
Helstone
Polyphant
South Petherwin
Lawhitton
Meadwell
Marystowe
Coryton
Rumps Point
Kellan Head
Varley Head
Port Quin Bay
Port Quin
Port Isaac
Port Gaverne
Lewannick
Kelly
Chillaton
Pentire Point
Padstow Bay
Hayle Bay
Trelights
Pendoggett
St Teath
Treveighan
Michaelstow
BROWN WILLY
Fivelanes
Trewint
Altarnun
Hexworthy
Bradstone
Milton Abbot
North Brentor
Stepper Point
Polzeath
Trebetherick
St Minver
St Endellion
Trelill
Trequite
Churchtown
St Breward
BODMIN MOOR
Illand
Trebullett
Lezant
Trekenner
Dunterton
Rezare
Bealsmill
Chaddlehanger
Lamerton
Mary Tavy
Trevose Head Heritage Coast
Mother Ivey's Bay
Harlyn Bay
Gunver Head
Rock
St Kew
St Kew Highway
St Tudy
Bolventor
North Hill
Middlewood
Coad's Green
Treburley
Kingston
Peter Tavy
Trevone
Harlyn
Windmill
Padstow
Chapel Amble
Bathpool
Bray Shop
Stoke Climsland
Sydenham Damerel
Horsebridge
Tavistock
St Merryn
Wadebridge
Egloshayle
St Mabyn
Blisland
Temple
SMALLACOMBE DOWNS
Henwood
Colliford Lake
Linkinhorne
Oldmill
Luckett
Latchley
Porthcothan
Penrose
Little Petherick
St Issey
Trenance
Royal Cornwall
Burlawn
Washaway
Helland
BROWNGELLY DOWNS
Minions
Upton
Billa Mill
South Hill
Downgate
Chilsworthy
Gulworthy
Whitchurch
St Ervan
Rumford
St Jidgey
Pencarrow House
Warleggan
Common Moor
Darite
Pensilva
Golberdon
Harrowbarrow
St Ann's Chapel
Gunnislake
St Eval
Camel Creek Adventure Park
Cardinham
Mount
St Neot
Tremar
St Cleer
Callington
Metherell
St Dominick
Albaston
Horrabridge
Nine Maidens
Rutherbridge
Frogwell
Calstock
Mawgan Porth
Nanstallon
Bodmin
Merrymeet
St Ive
Buckland Monachorum
St Mawgan
Rosenannon
St Wenn
Withiel
Talskiddy
Mellion
Bere Alston
Milton Combe

BRIDGWATER
BAY
EXMOOR FOREST
EXMOOR NATIONAL PARK
BRENDON HILLS
QUANTOCK HILLS
BLACKDOWN HILLS
DARTMOOR FOREST
DARTMOOR NATIONAL PARK
Lynton
Lynmouth
Countisbury
Porlock
Minehead
Dunster
Watchet
Barnstaple
South Molton
Dulverton
Bampton
Wellington
Taunton
Tiverton
Cullompton
Crediton
Exeter
Honiton
Ottery St Mary
Sidmouth
Budleigh Salterton
Exmouth
Topsham
Dawlish
Teignmouth
Newton Abbot
Kingsteignton
Bovey Tracey
Ashburton
Buckfastleigh
Kingskerswell
Okehampton
Chagford
Moretonhampstead
Seaton
Babbacombe Bay
Lyme Bay
Ladram Bay

14
WESTON-SUPER-MARE
BRIDGWATER
BAY
Burnham-on-Sea
Highbridge
Minehead
Watchet
Bridgwater
Glastonbury
Street
Cheddar
Wedmore
Winscombe
QUANTOCK HILLS
BRENDON HILLS
POLDEN HILLS
MENDIP HILLS
North Petherton
Taunton
Wellington
BLACKDOWN HILLS
Somerton
Martock
Ilminster
Crewkerne
Chard
Tiverton
Cullompton
Honiton
Axminster
Ottery St Mary
EXETER
Cranbrook
Topsham
Exmouth
Budleigh Salterton
Sidmouth
Seaton
Lyme Regis
Bridport
LYME BAY
Dawlish
Teignmouth
Kingskerswell
Babbacombe Bay
TORQUAY
5
3
B
C
D
E
F
G
H
J
K
1
2
3
4
5
6
7
8
9
10
11
12
13
14
15
16

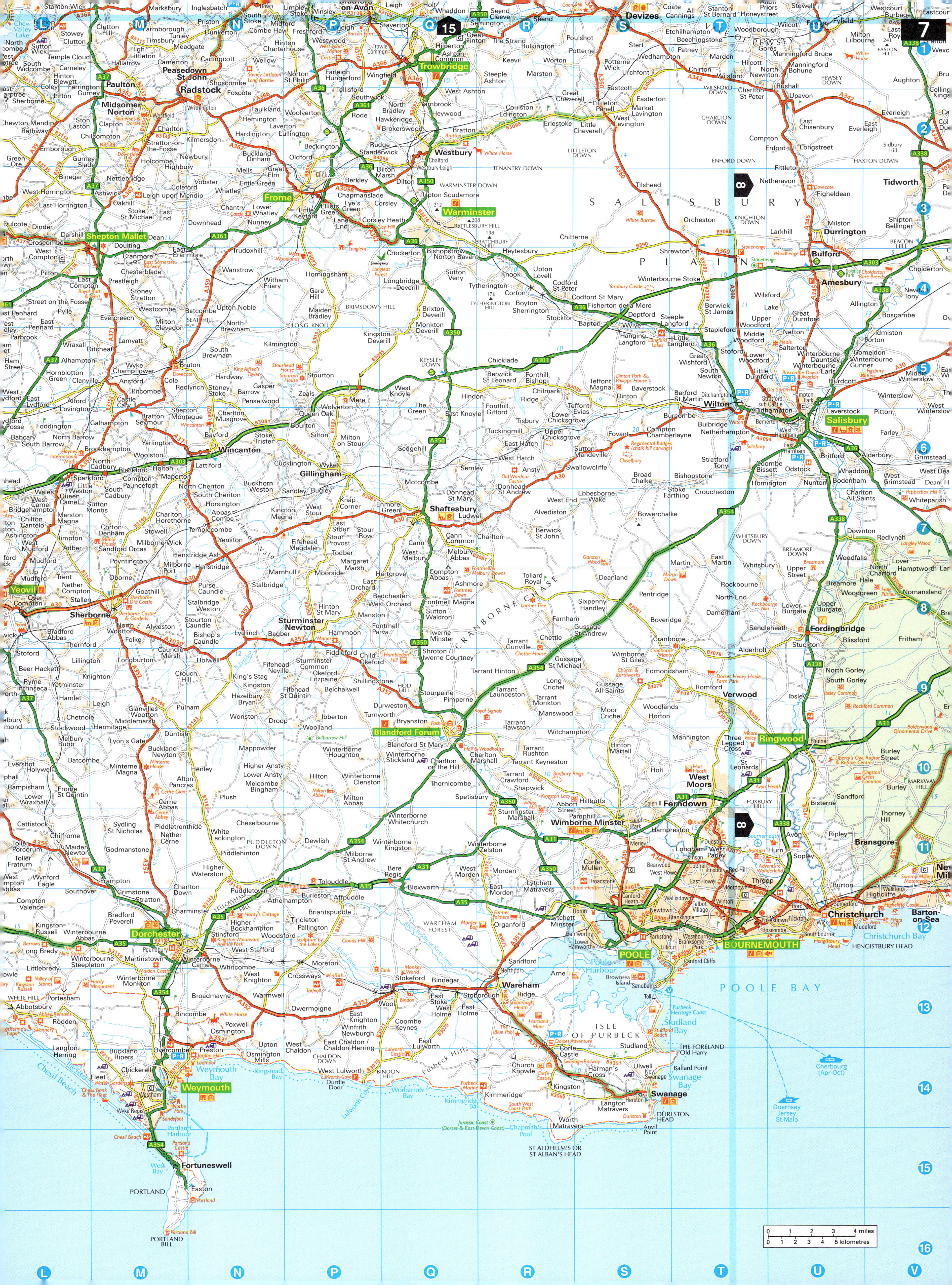
L
M
N
P
Q
R
S
T
U
V
15
8
Trowbridge
Frome
Westbury
Warminster
Shepton Mallet
Radstock
Devizes
Salisbury
Amesbury
Bulford
Durrington
Tidworth
Wilton
S A L I S B U R Y
P L A I N
Yeovil
Sherborne
Wincanton
Gillingham
Shaftesbury
Sturminster Newton
Blandford Forum
Fordingbridge
Ringwood
Verwood
Ferndown
West Moors
Wimborne Minster
Dorchester
Weymouth
Fortuneswell
PORTLAND
PORTLAND BILL
POOLE
BOURNEMOUTH
Christchurch
Wareham
Swanage
ISLE OF PURBECK
POOLE BAY
Chesil Beach
Weymouth Bay
Christchurch Bay
HENGISTBURY HEAD
Barton-on-Sea
Bransgore
CRANBORNE CHASE
DURLSTON HEAD
ST ALDHELM'S OR ST ALBAN'S HEAD
THE FORELAND Old Harry
Cherbourg (Apr-Oct)
Guernsey Jersey St-Malo
0 1 2 3 4 miles
0 1 2 3 4 5 kilometres

Devizes
Newbury
BASINGSTOKE
Andover
SALISBURY PLAIN
Amesbury
Salisbury
Wilton
Winchester
Romsey
EASTLEIGH
SOUTHAMPTON
Totton
Lyndhurst
NEW FOREST NATIONAL PARK
Fordingbridge
Ringwood
Ferndown
Wimborne Minster
POOLE
BOURNEMOUTH
Christchurch
Christchurch Bay
POOLE BAY
Poole Harbour
ISLE OF PURBECK
Swanage
Studland Bay
Lymington
New Milton
Milford on Sea
Hythe
Fawley
Fareham
GOSPORT
Portsmouth Harbour
THE SOLENT
Cowes
East Cowes
Yarmouth
Freshwater
Newport
Ryde
ISLE OF WIGHT
Shanklin
Sandown
Ventnor
Hedge End
Bishop's Waltham
Alresford
Whitchurch
Overton
Ludgershall
Tidworth
Stockbridge
Verwood
Brockenhurst
Sway
Hamble-le-Rice
Hengistbury Head
The Needles
Durlston Head
St Catherine's Point
Cherbourg (Apr-Oct)
Guernsey Jersey St-Malo

17
10
BRACKNELL
Crowthorne
Sandhurst
Bagshot
Windlesham
Lightwater
Chobham
Chertsey
Addlestone
Weybridge
Walton-on-Thames
Esher
Sutton
Epsom
Banstead
Byfleet
Cobham
Leatherhead
CAMBERLEY
Yateley
Fleet
Farnborough
Hook
Odiham
Aldershot
Farnham
Knaphill
WOKING
Ripley
East Horsley
GUILDFORD
Shalford
Godalming
Milford
Dorking
Reigate
Redhill
Horley
Salfords
Caterham
CRAWLEY
Horsham
Cranleigh
Haslemere
Hindhead
Grayshott
Bordon
Alton
Four Marks
Liphook
Liss
Petersfield
Midhurst
Billingshurst
Southwater
Pulborough
West Chiltington
Storrington
Steyning
Henfield
Hurstpierpoint
Hassocks
Burgess Hill
Arundel
Littlehampton
Angmering
WORTHING
Lancing
Shoreham-by-Sea
Portslade-by-Sea
HOVE
BRIGHTON
Chichester
BOGNOR REGIS
Middleton-on-Sea
Selsey
SELSEY BILL
Emsworth
HAVANT
Horndean
Waterlooville
Southsea
PORTSMOUTH
South Hayling
Hayling Island
Bembridge
FORELAND
Guernsey
Jersey
St-Malo
Caen (Ouistreham)
Cherbourg
Le Havre
Bilbao (Apr-Oct)
Santander
SOUTH DOWNS
NATIONAL PARK
M3
M25
M23
A3
A31
A272
A24
A27
A259
A29
A283
A285
A286
A281
A23
0 1 2 3 4 miles
0 1 2 3 4 5 kilometres
L
M
N
P
Q
R
S
T
U
1
2
3
4
5
6
7
8
9
10
11
12
13
14
15

10
17
18
9
B
C
D
E
F
G
H
J
K
Wembley
Camden Town
Islington
Hackney
Stratford
Barking
Rainham
South Ockendon
Stanford le Hope
Ealing
Hammersmith
LONDON
Greenwich
Woolwich
Aveley
Grays
Tilbury
Hounslow
Richmond
Brixton
Lewisham
Dartford
Northfleet
GRAVESEND
Kingston upon Thames
Wimbledon
Sunbury-on-Thames
Walton-on-Thames
Bromley
Swanley
Orpington
ROCHESTER
CHATHAM
Strood
Esher
Croydon
Sutton
New Addington
Eynsford
West Kingsdown
Meopham
Snodland
Epsom
Cobham
Banstead
Biggin Hill
Otford
Kemsing
Borough Green
Aylesford
Leatherhead
Warlingham
Caterham
Westerham
West Malling
Ditton
MAIDSTONE
Limpsfield
Oxted
Sevenoaks
East Horsley
Redhill
Godstone
Reigate
Dorking
Hildenborough
Tonbridge
Edenbridge
Coxheath
Lingfield
Horley
Southborough
Marden
Copthorne
East Grinstead
ROYAL TUNBRIDGE WELLS
Pembury
CRAWLEY
Crawley Down
Forest Row
Horsham
Crowborough
Wadhurst
Southwater
Billingshurst
Haywards Heath
Heathfield
Uckfield
Burgess Hill
Henfield
Hurstpierpoint
Hassocks
Steyning
Lewes
Hailsham
Battle
Bexhill-on-Sea
Shoreham-by-Sea
Southwick
Portslade-by-Sea
HOVE
BRIGHTON
WORTHING
Lancing
Sompting
Ferring
Rottingdean
Peacehaven
Newhaven
Seaford
Polegate
EASTBOURNE
Pevensey
Beachy Head
Dieppe
SOUTH DOWNS NATIONAL PARK
0 1 2 3 4 miles
0 1 2 3 4 5 kilometres

L
M
N
P
Q
R
S
T
U
V
1
2
3
4
5
6
7
8
9
10
11
12
13
14
15
16
19
Hadleigh
North Shoebury
Shoeburyness
SOUTHEND-ON-SEA
Shoebury Ness
Canvey Point
THAMES ESTUARY
Allhallows
Lower Stoke
Isle of Grain
Grain
Middle Stoke
Thamesport
Sheerness
Minster-on-Sea
Warden Point
Eastchurch
Leysdown-on-Sea
ISLE OF SHEPPEY
Queenborough
Rushenden
River Medway
Elmley Island
Isle of Harty
Shell Ness
The Swale
Rainham
Lower Halstow
Iwade
Upchurch
Newington
Bobbing
Sittingbourne
Hartlip
Borden
Bapchild
Teynham
Tunstall
Highsted
Rodmersham
Rodmersham Green
Faversham
Davington
Oare
Goodnestone
Graveney
Whitstable
Whitstable Bay
Seasalter
Herne Bay
Hampton
Tankerton
Swalecliffe
Beltinge
Greenhill
Bishopstone
Reculver
Minnis Bay
Birchington
Westgate-on-Sea
MARGATE
Foreness Point
Cliftonville
Kingsgate
NORTH FORELAND
Botany Bay
Joss Bay
Broadstairs
Ramsgate
Pegwell
Pegwell Bay
ISLE OF THANET
Lydden
Acol
Manston
Monkton
Minster
St Nicholas at-Wade
Sarre
Chislet
Boyden Gate
Hoath
Upstreet
West Stourmouth
East Stourmouth
Westmarsh
Herne
Broomfield
Yorkletts
Highstreet
Dargate
Denstroude
Hernhill
Staplestreet
Dunkirk
Blean
Upper Harbledown
Harbledown
Tyler Hill
Hales Place
Broad Oak
Sturry
Fordwich
Westbere
Hersden
Stodmarsh
Wickhambreaux
Preston
Elmstone
Canterbury
Thanington
Littlebourne
Ickham
Wingham
Durlock
Marshborough
Ash
Sandwich
Sandwich Bay
Woodnesborough
Staple
Goodnestone
Eastry
Worth
Ham
Hacklinge
Finglesham
Statenborough
Northbourne
Sholden
The Downs
Deal
Walmer
Ringwould
Kingsdown
St Margaret's at Cliffe
St Margaret's Bay
SOUTH FORELAND
West Cliffe
Guston
DOVER
Whitfield
Temple Ewell
Kearsney
River
Alkham
Capel-le-Ferne
Hougham
FOLKESTONE
Sandgate
Cheriton
Hythe
Seabrook
Saltwood
West Hythe
Palmarsh
Dymchurch
St Mary's Bay
Littlestone-on-Sea
Greatstone-on-Sea
New Romney
Lydd
DUNGENESS
The Old Lighthouse
Rye Bay
Camber
Rye
East Guldeford
Playden
Peasmarsh
Iden
Winchelsea
Icklesham
Guestling Thorn
Pett
Cliff End
Fairlight
HASTINGS
St Helen's
Baldslow
Westfield
Three Oaks
Guestling Green
Broad Street
Udimore
Cock Marling
Broad Oak
Brede
Broadland Row
Beckley
Clayhill
Northiam
Newenden
Sandhurst
Rolvenden
Rolvenden Layne
Tenterden
Small Hythe
Wittersham
ISLE OF OXNEY
Stone in Oxney
Appledore
Reading Street
Kenardington
Warehorne
Hamstreet
Ruckinge
Bilsington
Snave
Brenzett
Brenzett Green
Snargate
Brookland
Old Romney
Ivychurch
St Mary in the Marsh
Newchurch
Burmarsh
ROMNEY MARSH
WALLAND MARSH
Lympne
Aldington
Aldington Corner
Bonnington
Orlestone
Woodchurch
Shadoxhurst
Kingsnorth
Ashford
Mersham
Sevington
Smeeth
Sellindge
Stanford
Newington
Peene
Etchinghill
Postling
Paddlesworth
Hawkinge
Densole
Swingfield Minnis
Lyminge
Ottinge
Elham
Rhodes Minnis
Stowting
Brabourne
Brabourne Lees
Hastingleigh
Elmsted
Bodsham
Stelling Minnis
Waltham
Petham
Crundale
Wye
Brook
Hinxhill
Kennington
Boughton Lees
Boughton Aluph
Westwell
Charing
Challock
Molash
Godmersham
Chilham
Old Wives Lees
Selling
Chartham
Chartham Hatch
Shottenden
Badlesmere
Leaveland
Sheldwich
Throwley
Eastling
Stalisfield Green
Warren Street
Lenham
Lenham Heath
Harrietsham
Hollingbourne
Bearsted
Leeds
Broomfield
Eyhorne Street
Sutton Valence
Ulcombe
Grafty Green
Egerton
Little Chart
Pluckley
Pluckley Thorne
Hothfield
Great Chart
Smarden
Headcorn
Biddenden
Bethersden
High Halden
Three Chimneys
Frinsted
Wormshill
Bicknor
Hucking
Doddington
Newnham
Milstead
Bredgar
Stockbury
Wichling
Tong
Lynsted
Ospringe
Painter's Forstal
North Street
Hogben's Hill
Boughton Street
South Street
Oversland
Nackington
Street End
Lower Hardres
Bridge
Bishopsbourne
Patrixbourne
Bekesbourne
Adisham
Aylesham
Womenswold
Kingston
Barham
Derringstone
Bossingham
Denton
Selsted
Wootton
Lydden
Shepherdswell
Coldred
Eythorne
Barfrestone
Tilmanstone
Elvington
Nonington
Chillenden
Ratling
Betteshanger
Great Mongeham
Sutton
East Studdal
Ashley
Martin
West Langdon
East Langdon
Ripple
Channel Tunnel (Rail)
STRAIT OF DOVER
Calais Dunkirk
M2
M20
A2
A20
A28
A249
A299
A252
A251
A256
A259
A262
A268
A2070

Cardigan Island
Ceredigion Heritage Coast
Mwnt Beach
Cardigan Island Coastal Farm
Y Ferwig
Aberporth
Tresaith
Llangranog
Penbryn
Blaenannerch
Tan-y-groes
Blaenporth
Tremain
Penparc
Beulah
Poppit Sands
Pembrokeshire Coast Path
St Dogmaels
Cardigan
(Aberteifi)
St Dogmaels Moylegrove Heritage Coast
Moylegrove
Ponthirwaun
Llechryd
Llandygwydd
TIVY SIDE
Cilgerran
Pen-y-bryn
Castle
Welsh Wildlife Centre
Teifi Marshes
Abercych
Cenarth
National Coracle Centre
Newcastle Emlyn
(Castell Newydd Emlyn)
Rhoshill
Pen-rhiw
Newchapel
Boncath
Blaenffos
Capel Iwan
Bwlch-y-groes
Star
Tegryn
Hermon
Llanfyrnach
Trelech
Glandwr
Hebron
Blaenwaun
Cwmbach
Llanwinio
Cefn-y-pant
Login
Llanboidy
Gellywen
Meidrim
Efailwen
Llandissilio
Llanfallteg
Llanfallteg West
Clunderwen
Cwmfelin Boeth
Llangynin
Whitland Abbey
Whitland
Pwll-trap
St Clears
(Sancler)
Llanddewi Velfrey
Lampeter Velfrey
Crinow
Tavernspite
Llanddowror
Red Roses
Ludchurch
Llanteg
Llansadurnen
Pendine
Llanmiloe
Colby Woodland Garden
Amroth
Stepaside
Kilgetty
Summerhill
Wiseman's Bridge
Copper Hall
Saundersfoot
Monkstone Point
New Hedges
Tenby
(Dinbych-y-pysgod)
Penally
Giltar Point
(May-Sept)
CALDEY ISLAND
CARMARTHEN BAY
Rosslare
STRUMBLE HEAD
Pen Brush
Carregwastad Head
Dinas Head Heritage Coast
DINAS HEAD
Newport Bay
Trwyn y bwa
Fishguard Bay
Llanwnda
Goodwick
(Wdig)
Fishguard
(Abergwaun)
Trefasser
Pwll Deri
Manorowen
St Nicholas
Granston
Abercastle
Ynys Dauliyn
Carreg Sampson
Porthgain
Trefin
Mathry
Llangloffan
Abereiddy
Berea
Llanrhian
Croes-goch
Treglemais
ST DAVID'S HEAD
Treleddyd-fawr
Whitesands Bay
Rhodiad-y-brenin
Caer Farchell
Whitchurch
RAMSEY ISLAND
Ramsey Sound
St Davids
(Tyddewi)
Bishop's Palace
Solva
St David's Peninsula Heritage Coast
Newgale
Penycwm
Roch
Llandeloy
Treffgarne Owen
Hayscastle
Hayscastle Cross
Wolf's Castle
Treffgarne
Letterston
Jordanston
Scleddau
Trecwn
Little Newcastle
Llanychaer
Mynydd Melyn
MYNYDD CAREGOG
Pontfaen
Pentre Ifan
Dinas Cross
Bryn-Henllan
Newport
Nevern
Felindre Farchog
Castell Henllys
Eglwyswrw
Crosswell
Brynberian
Crymych
Foel Drygarn
PEMBROKESHIRE COAST
MYNYDD PRESELI
NATIONAL PARK
FOEL CWMCERWYN
Mynachlog ddu
FOEL DRYCH
Rosebush
Puncheston
Castlebythe
Tufton
Maenclochog
Llangolman
Llandre Isaf
Llanglydwen
Henry's Moat
(Castell Hendre)
Llys-y-frân Reservoir
Llys-y-frân
New Moat
Pen-ffordd
Llanycefn
Rinaston
Ambleston
Spittal
Scolton Manor
Walton East
Clarbeston
Clarbeston Road
Bletherston
DUDWELL MOUNTAIN
Leweston
Wolfsdale
Camrose
PEMBROKESHIRE COAST NATIONAL PARK
Rickets Head
Nolton Haven
Nolton
Simpson Cross
Keeston
St Brides Bay
St Brides Bay Heritage Coast
Druidston
Haroldston West
Broad Haven
Little Haven
Portfield Gate
Broadway
Walton West
Haverfordwest
(Hwlffordd)
Pembrokeshire County
Fenton Brook
Wiston
Llawhaden
Robeston Wathen
Bethesda
Narberth
(Arberth)
Uzmaston
Dreen Hill
Picton Castle
Bluestone
Oakwood
Templeton
Martletwy
Talbenny
Wooltack Point
Lockley Lodge
SKOMER ISLAND
(Apr-Sept)
Marloes
Tiers Cross
Walwyn's Castle
Freystrop
Johnston
Hook
Llangwm
Rosemarket
St Ishmael's
Broad Sound
Marloes & Dale Heritage Coast
Westdale Bay
Dale
SKOKHOLM ISLAND
Dale Point
Great Castle Head
Herbrandston
Hubberston
Steynton
Waterston
Llanstadwell
Milford Haven
(Aberdaugleddau)
Houghton
Burton
Lawrenny
West Williamston
Cresswell
Loveston
Reynalton
Begelly
Jeffreyston
Broadmoor
Neyland
Pembroke Dock
(Doc Penfro)
Cosheston
Carew
Carew Newton
Milton
Redberth
East Williamston
Heatherton World of Activities
Sageston
Cheriton
St Florence
Gumfreston
Manorbier Newton
Manor House
Angle
Angle Bay
Chapel Bay Fort
St Ann's Head
Rhoscrowther
Pembroke
(Penfro)
Lamphey
Bishop's Palace
Manorbier
Hundleton
Maiden Wells
Hodgeston
Jameston
Lydstep
Lydstep Point
Freshwater West
Castlemartin Brook
Castlemartin
Warren
St Twynnells
Merrion
Freshwater East
Trewent Point
Stackpole Elidor
Cheriton
Linney Head
PEMBROKESHIRE COAST NATIONAL PARK
Stackpole
Bosherston
Elegug Stacks
Stackpole Head
St Govan's Chapel
St Govan's Head
South Pembrokeshire Heritage Coast
0 1 2 3 4 miles
0 1 2 3 4 5 kilometres

Lampeter (Llanbedr Pont Steffan)
Llandovery (Llanymddyfri)
Carmarthen (Caerfyrddin)
Llandeilo
Ammanford (Rhydaman)
Kidwelly (Cydweli)
Llanelli
Burry Port (Porth Tywyn)
Gorseinon
Pontarddulais
Clydach
Pontardawe
Neath (Castell-nedd)
SWANSEA (ABERTAWE)
Port Talbot
Bridgend (Pen-y-bont-ar-Ogwr)
Porthcawl
Maesteg
Aberdare (Aberdâr)
Hirwaun
Llantwit Major (Llanilltud Fawr)
Cowbridge
Sennybridge
Builth Road
BANNAU BRYCHEINIOG (BRECON BEACONS)
NATIONAL PARK
BLACK MOUNTAIN
FFOREST FAWR
Mynydd Eppynt
Swansea Bay
Oxwich Bay
Rhossili Bay
Burry Inlet
Broughton Bay
Vale of Neath
Afan Forest Park
Rhondda Valley
Mumbles Head
The Mumbles
Worms Head
Gower Heritage Coast
Glamorgan Heritage Coast
M4
A40
A48
A483
A465
A470
A4069
L
M
N
P
Q
R
S
T
U
V
1
2
3
4
5
6
7
8
9
10
11
12
13
14
15
16
20
14

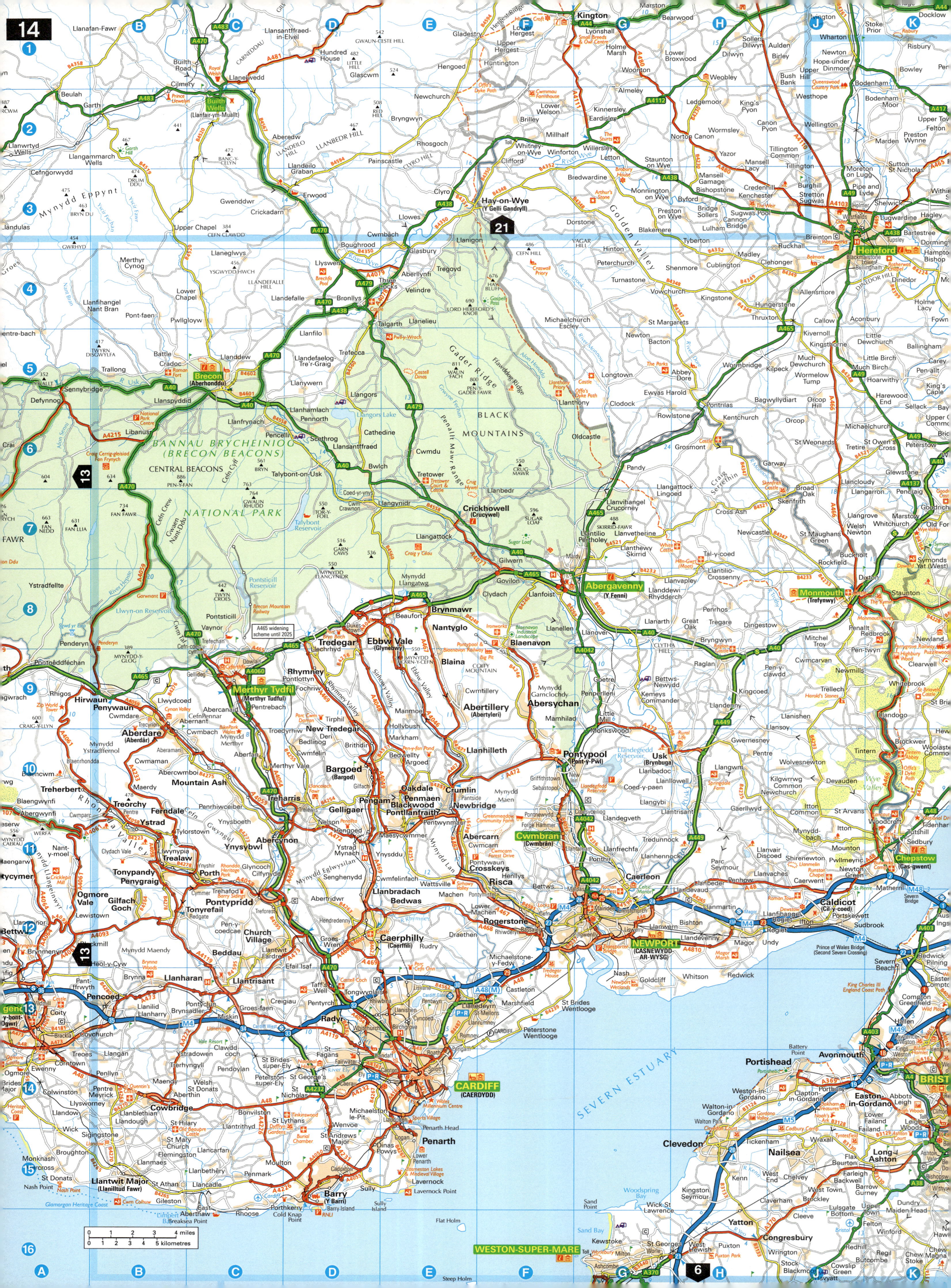
Builth Wells
Kington
Hay-on-Wye
Hereford
Brecon
Bannau Brycheiniog (Brecon Beacons) National Park
Central Beacons
Black Mountains
Golden Valley
Crickhowell
Abergavenny
Monmouth
Merthyr Tydfil
Ebbw Vale
Tredegar
Brynmawr
Blaenavon
Aberdare
Mountain Ash
Pontypool
Usk
Cwmbran
Caerphilly
Pontypridd
Newport
Cardiff
Chepstow
Caldicot
Barry
Penarth
Cowbridge
Llantwit Major
Pencoed
Portishead
Clevedon
Nailsea
Weston-super-Mare
Severn Estuary
Avonmouth
Bristol
0 1 2 3 4 miles
0 1 2 3 4 5 kilometres

22
23
15
16
7
8
WORCESTER
Stratford-upon-Avon
Malvern
Pershore
Evesham
Ledbury
Broadway
Chipping Campden
Tewkesbury
Moreton-in-Marsh
Bishop's Cleeve
Winchcombe
Ross-on-Wye
Newent
Stow-on-the-Wold
CHELTENHAM
Charlton Kings
GLOUCESTER
Bourton-on-the-Water
Cinderford
Brockworth
Stroud
Stonehouse
Lydney
Chalford
Cirencester
Minchinhampton
Nailsworth
Dursley
River Severn
Wotton-under-Edge
Tetbury
Cricklade
Highworth
Faringdon
Carterton
Malmesbury
Purton
SWINDON
Royal Wootton Bassett
Wroughton
Yate
Chipping Sodbury
Chippenham
Calne
Corsham
Keynsham
BATH
Melksham
Bradford-on-Avon
Devizes
Marlborough
Shipston-on-Stour

16
23
24
15
8
Stratford-upon-Avon
Wellesbourne
Banbury
Brackley
Buckingham
Towcester
Newport Pagnell
Stony Stratford
MILTON KEYNES
Winslow
Bicester
Kidlington
OXFORD
Witney
Carterton
Chipping Norton
Stow-on-the-Wold
Shipston-on-Stour
Moreton-in-Marsh
Aylesbury
Thame
Wheatley
Princes Risborough
Chinnor
Abingdon-on-Thames
Didcot
Wantage
Wallingford
Faringdon
Henley-on-Thames
Marlow
READING
Wokingham
Newbury
Hungerford
Marlborough
Thatcham
Goring
Benson
Watlington
Stokenchurch
Eynsham
Woodstock
Bampton
Grove
Cholsey
Earley
Binfield
Twyford
Wargrave
Sandhurst
Crowthorne
Shinfield
Theale
Tadley
LAMBOURN DOWNS
M40
M4
A329(M)
A404(M)

17
25
18
10
9
Bedford
Kempston
Biggleswade
Sandy
Potton
Gamlingay
Royston
Melbourn
Great Shelford
Sawston
Saffron Walden
Fulbourn
Linton
Ampthill
Flitwick
Shefford
Henlow
Stotfold
Baldock
Letchworth Garden City
Hitchin
Stevenage
Knebworth
Buntingford
Bishop's Stortford
Stansted Mountfitchet
Sawbridgeworth
Harlow
Epping
Ware
Hertford
Welwyn Garden City
Welwyn
Hatfield
Hoddesdon
Cheshunt
Waltham Abbey
Potters Bar
Enfield
Barnet
Borehamwood
Radlett
St Albans
Harpenden
Luton
Dunstable
Houghton Regis
Leighton Buzzard
Woburn Sands
Tring
Berkhamsted
Hemel Hempstead
Kings Langley
Watford
Chesham
Amersham
Rickmansworth
Chalfont St Peter
Beaconsfield
Slough
Uxbridge
Windsor
Eton
Staines-upon-Thames
Egham
Chertsey
Weybridge
Walton-on-Thames
Sunbury-on-Thames
Hounslow
Richmond
Kingston upon Thames
Wimbledon
Harrow
Wembley
Ealing
Hammersmith
Camden Town
Islington
Hackney
Stratford
Barking
Romford
Chigwell
LONDON
Greenwich
Woolwich
Brixton
Lewisham
Bromley
Croydon
Sutton
Dartford
Swanley
Orpington
Sevenoaks
Esher
Epsom
Ascot
Addlestone
Virginia Water
Rainham
Aveley

18
Huntingdon
St Ives
Haddenham
Mildenhall
Thetford Forest Park
Brampton
Godmanchester
Soham
St Neots
Cottenham
Waterbeach
26
Burwell
Newmarket
Bury St Edmunds
Histon
Girton
Milton
CAMBRIDGE
25
Cambourne
Fulbourn
Great Shelford
Sawston
Linton
Haverhill
Long Melford
Sudbury
Biggleswade
Potton
Melbourn
17
Royston
Saffron Walden
Stotfold
Baldock
Letchworth Garden City
Sible Hedingham
Halstead
Buntingford
STEVENAGE
Braintree
Coggeshall
Stansted Mountfitchet
Bishop's Stortford
Great Dunmow
Great Notley
Kelvedon
Knebworth
Ware
Sawbridgeworth
Welwyn
Welwyn Garden City
Hertford
Witham
HARLOW
Hatfield
Hoddesdon
Hatfield Peverel
Writtle
CHELMSFORD
Maldon
Danbury
Cheshunt
Waltham Abbey
Epping
North Weald Bassett
Chipping Ongar
Potters Bar
Enfield
Theydon Bois
Ingatestone
Barnet
Chigwell
BRENTWOOD
Billericay
Wickford
Rayleigh
Hockley
Hullbridge
Romford
BASILDON
Hadleigh
South Benfleet
Barking
Stratford
Hackney
Camden Town
Islington
Rainham
South Ockendon
Stanford le Hope
10
Canvey Island
THAMES ESTUARY
M11
M25
A1(M)
A14
A120
A12
A127
A13

Southwold
Blythburgh
Walberswick
Halesworth
Wenhaston
Dunwich
Westleton
Yoxford
Middleton
Theberton
Eastbridge
Kelsale
Saxmundham
Leiston
Aldringham
Thorpeness
Aldeburgh
Aldeburgh Bay
Snape
Framlingham
Saxtead Green
Dennington
Wickham Market
Woodbridge
Melton
Ufford
Orford
Orford Ness
Butley
Sudbourne
Hollesley
Hollesley Bay
Shottisham
Bawdsey
Alderton
Martlesham Heath
Martlesham
Kesgrave
IPSWICH
Felixstowe
Landguard Point
Harwich
Dovercourt
Parkeston
Hook of Holland
Manningtree
Mistley
Lawford
Dedham
Brantham
Holbrook
Shotley Gate
COLCHESTER
Wivenhoe
Brightlingsea
West Mersea
Mersea Island
East Mersea
Tiptree
Tollesbury
Jaywick
CLACTON-ON-SEA
St Osyth
Frinton-on-Sea
Walton-on-the-Naze
The Naze
Hamford Water
Pennyhole Bay
Great Oakley
Little Oakley
Ramsey
Thorpe-le-Soken
Kirby-le-Soken
Weeley
Great Bentley
Alresford
Stowmarket
Needham Market
Hadleigh
Boxford
Nayland
Bildeston
Debenham
Eye
Mendlesham
Coddenham
Claydon
Capel St Mary
East Bergholt
Southminster
Burnham-on-Crouch
Bradwell-on-Sea
Bradwell Waterside
St Lawrence
Mayland
Steeple
Dengie
Tillingham
Foulness Island
Foulness Point
Canewdon
Paglesham
Great Wakering
North Shoebury
Shoeburyness
Shoebury Ness
River Blackwater
River Stour
River Orwell
Colne Point
Sales Point
Holliwell Point
A12
A14
A120
A133
A140
A1120
A1094
A1156
A1214
27
11
L
M
N
P
Q
R
S
T
U
V
1
2
3
4
5
6
7
8
9
10
11
12
13
14
15
16
0 1 2 3 4 miles
0 1 2 3 4 5 kilometres

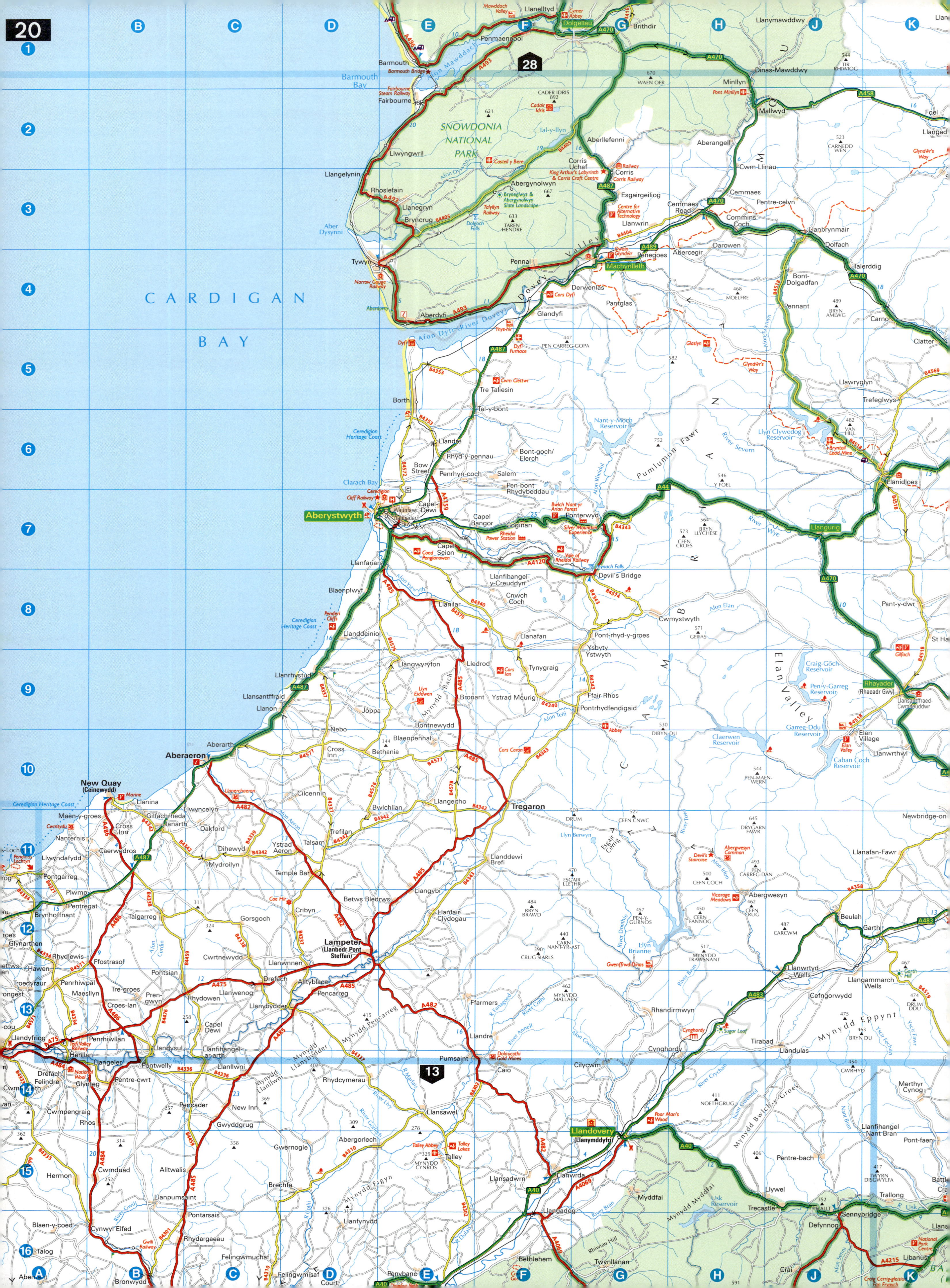
CARDIGAN
BAY
SNOWDONIA
NATIONAL
PARK
Dolgellau
Llanelltyd
Cymer Abbey
Brithdir
Llanymawddwy
Penmaenpool
Barmouth
Barmouth Bridge
Barmouth Bay
Fairbourne Steam Railway
Fairbourne
CADER IDRIS 892
Cadair Idris
Tal-y-llyn
Llwyngwril
Castell y Bere
Llangelynin
Rhoslefain
Llanegryn
Bryncrug
Abergynolwyn
Corris Uchaf
Corris
Corris Railway
King Arthur's Labyrinth & Corris Craft Centre
Aberllefenni
Talyllyn Railway
Dolgoch Falls
TAREN HENDRE
Aber Dysynni
Tywyn
Narrow Gauge Railway
Aberdovey
Aberdyfi
Pennal
Dinas-Mawddwy
Minllyn
Pont Minllyn
Mallwyd
WAEN OER
Aberangell
Cwm-Llinau
Esgairgeiliog
Centre for Alternative Technology
Llanwrin
Cemmaes
Cemmaes Road
Commins Coch
Pentre-celyn
Llanbrynmair
Dolfach
Darowen
Abercegir
Penegoes
Machynlleth
Dyfi Valley
Derwenlas
Pantglas
Glandyfi
Cors Dyfi
Ynys-hir
Dyfi Furnace
PEN CARREG-GOPA
MOELFRE
Bont-Dolgadfan
Pennant
Talerddig
Carno
Clatter
Foel
Llangadfan
Glyndŵr's Way
Afon Dyfi (River Dovey)
Glaslyn
Cwm Clettwr
Tre Taliesin
Tal-y-bont
Borth
Ceredigion Heritage Coast
Llandre
Bow Street
Rhyd-y-pennau
Penrhyn-coch
Bont-goch/ Elerch
Salem
Pen-bont Rhydybeddau
Nant-y-Moch Reservoir
Pumlumon Fawr
River Severn
Llyn Clywedog Reservoir
Llawryglyn
Trefeglwys
Llanidloes
Bryntail Lead Mine
VAN HILL
Y FOEL
Clarach Bay
Aberystwyth
Cliff Railway
Capel-Dewi
Capel Bangor
Goginan
Bwlch Nant yr Arian Forest
Ponterwyd
Silver Mountain Experience
Rheidol Power Station
Vale of Rheidol Railway
Capel Seion
Coed Penglanowen
Llanfarian
Devil's Bridge
Llanfihangel-y-Creuddyn
Cnwch Coch
Blaenplwyf
Llanilar
Llanafan
Pont-rhyd-y-groes
Ysbyty Ystwyth
Cwmystwyth
River Wye
Llangurig
Pant-y-dwr
Afon Elan
Llanddeiniol
Penderi Cliffs
Llangwyryfon
Lledrod
Cors Fochno
Tynygraig
Llanrhystud
Llansantffraid
Llanon
Llyn Eiddwen
Mynydd Bach
Bronant
Ystrad Meurig
Ffair Rhos
Pontrhydfendigaid
Strata Florida Abbey
Joppa
Nebo
Bontnewydd
Blaenpennal
Bethania
Cross Inn
Aberarth
Aberaeron
Cors Caron
New Quay (Ceinewydd)
Llanina
Ceredigion Heritage Coast
Maen-y-groes
Gilfachrheda
Llanarth
Llwyncelyn
Oakford
Cilcennin
Llangeitho
Bwlchllan
Tregaron
Nanternis
Caerwedros
Dihewyd
Ystrad Aeron
Trefilan
Talsarn
Mydroilyn
Temple Bar
Llanddewi Brefi
Llwyndafydd
Pontgarreg
Plwmp
Pentregat
Brynhoffnant
Talgarreg
Gorsgoch
Cribyn
Betws Bledrws
Llangybi
Llanfair Clydogau
Lampeter (Llanbedr Pont Steffan)
Rhydlewis
Ffostrasol
Cwrtnewydd
Llanwnnen
Pontsian
Drefach
Alltyblaca
Llanwenog
Pencarreg
Llanybydder
Rhydowen
Tre-groes
Penrhiwpal
Maesllyn
Croes-lan
Pren-gwyn
Capel Dewi
Mynydd Pencarreg
Ffarmers
Llandre
Pumsaint
Dolaucothi Gold Mines
Caio
Cilycwm
Cynghordy
Sugar Loaf
Llandyfriog
Penrhiwllan
Henllan
Teifi Valley Railway
Llandysul
Llangeler
Pontwelly
Llanfihangel-ar-arth
Llanllwni
Drefach Felindre
National Wool Museum
Pentre-cwrt
Rhydcymerau
Llansawel
Abergorlech
Talley Abbey
Talley
Talley Lakes
Pencader
New Inn
Gwyddgrug
Cwmpengraig
Rhos
Gwernogle
Hermon
Cwmduad
Alltwalis
Brechfa
Llansadwrn
Llanwrda
Llandovery (Llanymddyfri)
Poor Man's Wood
Myddfai
Llangadog
Usk Reservoir
Mynydd Myddfai
Mynydd Figyn
Llanpumsaint
Pontarsais
Rhydargaeau
Llanfynydd
Blaen-y-coed
Cynwyl Elfed
Gwili Railway
Talog
Felingwmuchaf
Felingwmisaf
Court
Bronwydd
Bethlehem
Twynllanan
Penybanc
Trecastle
Sennybridge
Defynnog
Crai
Libanus
National Park Centre
Trallong
Llywel
Pentre-bach
Llanfihangel Nant Bran
Pont-faen
Merthyr Cynog
Mynydd Bwlch-y-Groes
NOETHGRUG
GWRHYD
Tirabad
Llandulas
Mynydd Eppynt
Cefngorwydd
Llanwrtyd Wells
Llangammarch Wells
Garth
Beulah
Rhandirmwyn
Gwenffrwd-Dinas
Llyn Brianne
Abergwesyn
Abergwesyn Common
Devil's Staircase
Llanafan-Fawr
Newbridge-on-Wye
Elan Valley
Craig-Goch Reservoir
Pen-y-Garreg Reservoir
Garreg-Ddu Reservoir
Claerwen Reservoir
Caban Coch Reservoir
Elan Village
Rhayader (Rhaeadr Gwy)
Llansantffraed-Cwmdeuddwr
Llanwrthwl
Gilfach
Llyn Berwyn
CAMBRIAN MOUNTAINS

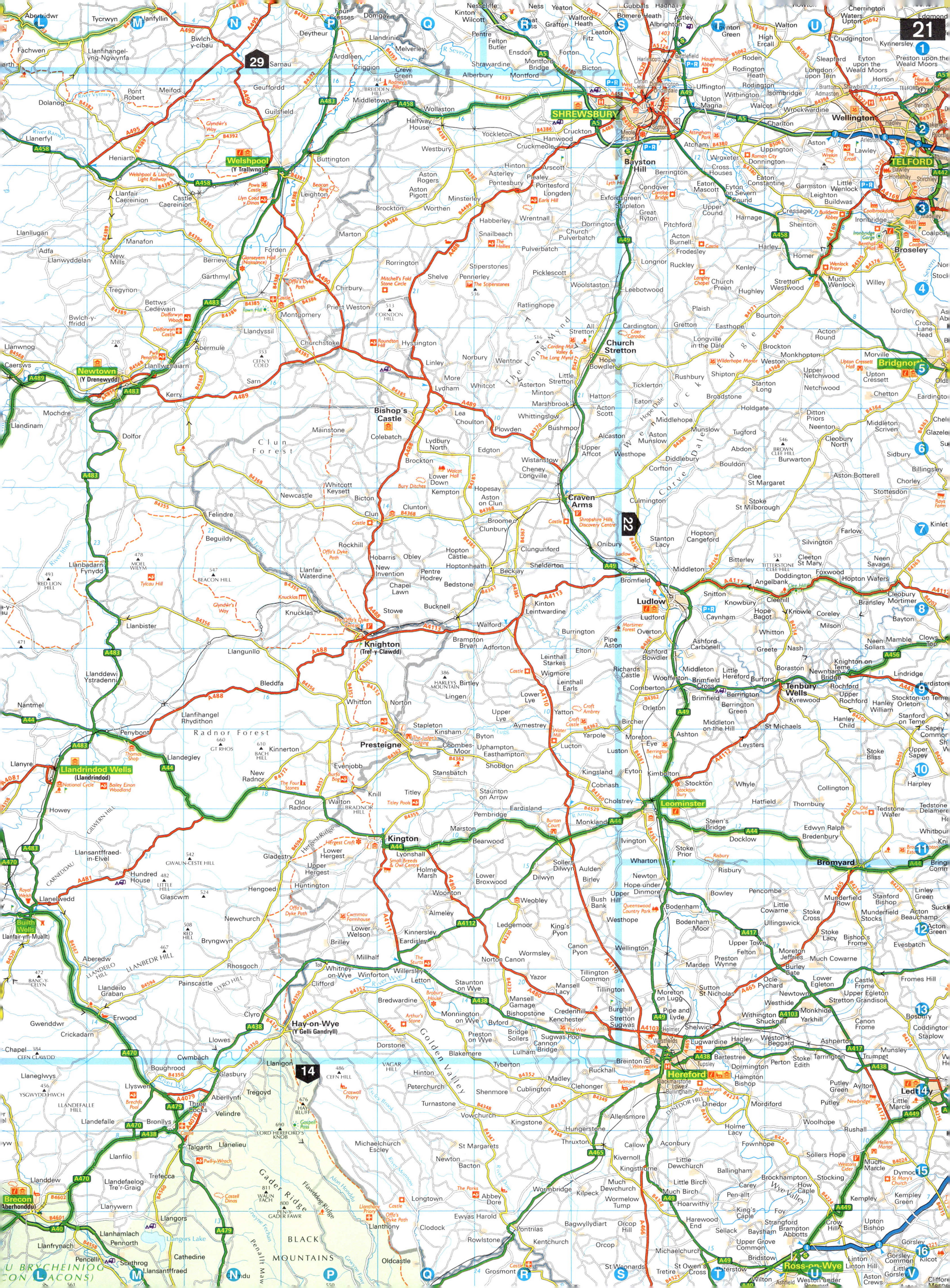
Shrewsbury
Wellington
Telford
Welshpool (Y Trallwng)
Newtown (Y Drenewydd)
Bridgnorth
Church Stretton
Bishop's Castle
Craven Arms
Ludlow
Knighton (Tref-y-Clawdd)
Presteigne
Llandrindod Wells (Llandrindod)
Kington
Leominster
Tenbury Wells
Bromyard
Builth Wells (Llanfair-ym-Muallt)
Hay-on-Wye (Y Gelli Gandryll)
Hereford
Ledbury
Ross-on-Wye
Brecon (Aberhonddu)
Broseley
Much Wenlock
Bayston Hill
Montgomery
Clun
Clun Forest
Radnor Forest
Golden Valley
The Long Mynd
Wenlock Edge
Corve Dale
Black Mountains
Gader Ridge
Wye Valley
A5
A49
A483
A44
A438
A458
A489
A488
A470
A4113
29
22
14

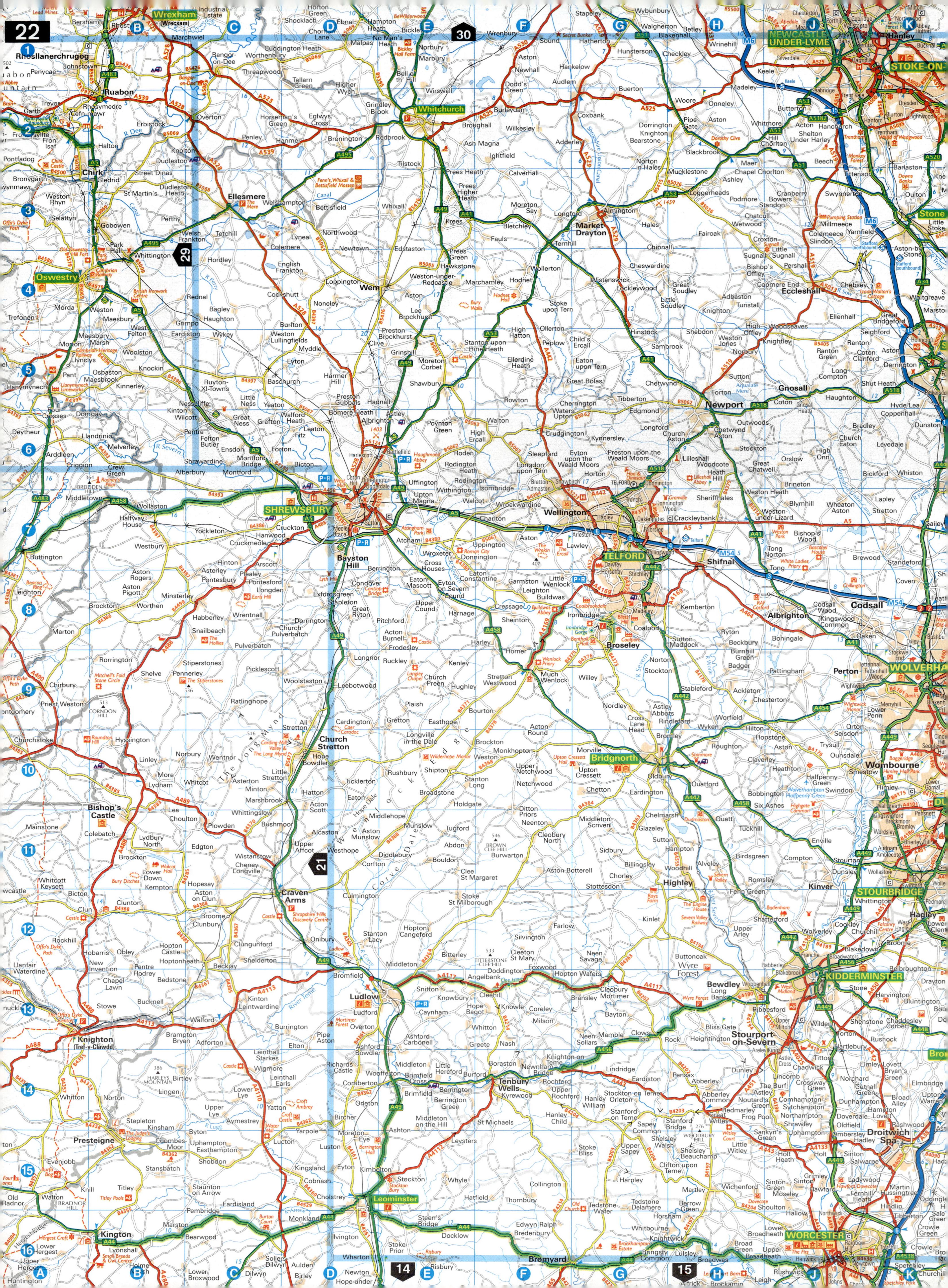

30
29
21
14
15
Wrexham (Wrecsam)
Rhosllanerchrugog
Ruabon
Chirk
Oswestry
Ellesmere
Whitchurch
Market Drayton
Newcastle-under-Lyme
Stoke-on-Trent
Hanley
Stone
Eccleshall
Newport
Gnosall
Shrewsbury
Wellington
Telford
Shifnal
Codsall
Albrighton
Bayston Hill
Broseley
Ironbridge
Much Wenlock
Church Stretton
Bridgnorth
Wombourne
Perton
Kinver
Stourbridge
Bishop's Castle
Craven Arms
Clun
Knighton (Tref-y-Clawdd)
Ludlow
Tenbury Wells
Bewdley
Kidderminster
Stourport-on-Severn
Droitwich Spa
Presteigne
Kington
Leominster
Bromyard
Worcester
Highley
Cleobury Mortimer
Wem
The Long Mynd
Wenlock Edge
Corve Dale
Wyre Forest

31
32
24
15
16
NOTTINGHAM
DERBY
Ashbourne
Uttoxeter
BURTON UPON TRENT
Swadlincote
Ashby-de-la-Zouch
Loughborough
Coalville
Shepshed
Rugeley
Lichfield
CANNOCK
Brownhills
TAMWORTH
WALSALL
WEST BROMWICH
BIRMINGHAM
SOLIHULL
REDDITCH
Warwick
ROYAL LEAMINGTON SPA
Stratford upon Avon
COVENTRY
NUNEATON
Hinckley
LEICESTER
RUGBY
Daventry
Kenilworth
Atherstone
Bedworth
Lutterworth
Kidderminster
Hednesford
Melbourne
Beeston
West Bridgford
Long Eaton
Ilkeston
Heanor
Belper
Eastwood
Hucknall
Stapleford
Uttoxeter
Tutbury
Hilton
Polesworth
Coleshill
Knowle
Studley
Alcester
Henley-in-Arden
Wellesbourne
Southam
Birstall
Wigston
Blaby
Enderby
Earl Shilton
Kirby Muxloe
Ratby
Anstey
Mountsorrel
Rothley
Sileby
Quorn
Whitwick
Ibstock
Measham
Castle Donington
Kegworth
Cheadle
Stone
Burntwood
Aldridge
ROYAL SUTTON COLDFIELD
Smethwick
HALESOWEN
Romsley
Alvechurch
Hockley Heath
Dorridge

32
23
16
NOTTINGHAM
DERBY
LEICESTER
COVENTRY
NORTHAMPTON
BURTON UPON TRENT
Loughborough
Melton Mowbray
Hinckley
NUNEATON
RUGBY
ROYAL LEAMINGTON SPA
Warwick
Market Harborough
Kettering
CORBY
Wellingborough
Oakham
Daventry
Kenilworth
Bedworth
Coalville
Ashby-de-la-Zouch
Swadlincote
Ilkeston
Long Eaton
Beeston
West Bridgford
Hucknall
Arnold
Belper
Heanor
Eastwood
Stapleford
Castle Donington
Shepshed
Oadby
Wigston
Lutterworth
Atherstone
Uppingham
Bingham
Ruddington
Syston
Birstall
Rothwell
Desborough
Burton Latimer
Irthlingborough
Earls Barton
Brixworth
Southam
M1
M6
M69
M42
M45
A14
A46
A5
A6
A47
A43
A52
A45
A38
A50
A606
A607
A4304
A5199
A426
A444
A453
A4303
A427
A428
A425
A508
A509
A6003
A6116
A4114
A447
A512
A514
A516
A444
A423
A361
A4177

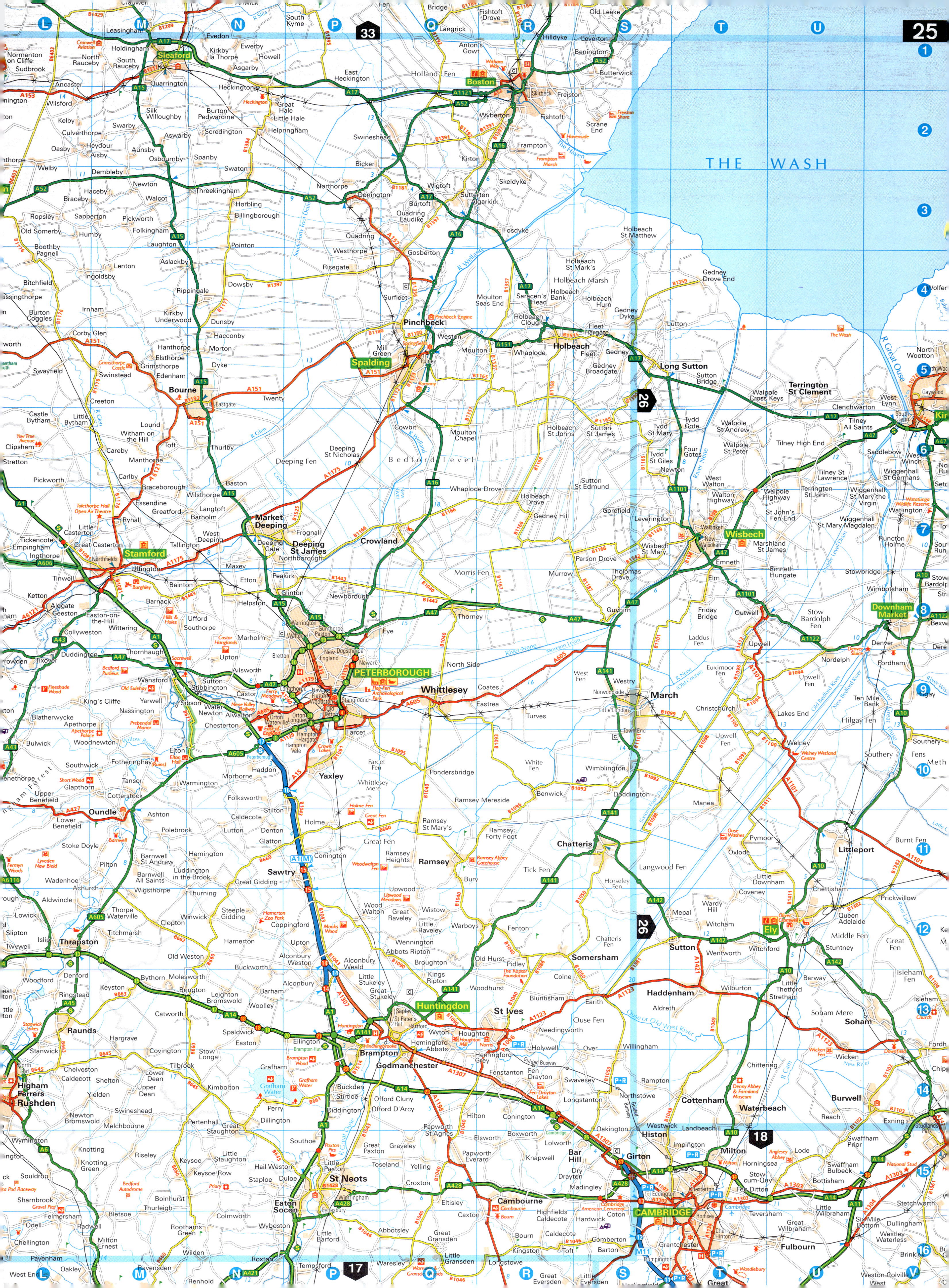
THE WASH
Sleaford
Boston
Spalding
Pinchbeck
Holbeach
Long Sutton
Bourne
Market Deeping
Deeping St James
Stamford
Crowland
PETERBOROUGH
Whittlesey
Wisbech
March
Downham Market
Oundle
Yaxley
Ramsey
Chatteris
Littleport
Ely
Huntingdon
St Ives
Somersham
Haddenham
Sutton
Soham
Thrapston
Raunds
Higham Ferrers
Rushden
Brampton
Godmanchester
St Neots
Cambourne
Cottenham
Waterbeach
CAMBRIDGE
Fulbourn
Girton
Milton
Histon
Sawtry
Kimbolton
Eaton Socon
Bedford Level
Holbeach Marsh
Terrington St Clement
Upwell
Outwell
Emneth
Thorney
Eye
Burwell
A1
A1(M)
A14
A15
A16
A17
A47
A141
A142
A151
A605
A1101
A1123
A1307
M11
33
26
18
17

33
THE WASH
Boston
Spalding
Pinchbeck
Holbeach
Long Sutton
Terrington St Clement
King's Lynn
Hunstanton
Heacham
Dersingham
Snettisham
Sandringham
Castle Rising
Brancaster
Burnham Market
Swaffham
Downham Market
Wisbech
March
Whittlesey
PETERBOROUGH
Crowland
Thorney
Chatteris
Ramsey
Huntingdon
St Ives
Somersham
Littleport
Ely
Soham
Mildenhall
Brandon
Thetford
Thetford Forest Park
Lakenheath
Feltwell
Methwold
Newmarket
Bury St Edmunds
CAMBRIDGE
Histon
Girton
Cottenham
Waterbeach
Burwell
Haddenham
Sutton
St Neots
Godmanchester
Brampton
Cambourne
Fulbourn
Yaxley
Bedford Level
25
18

L
M
N
P
Q
R
S
T
U
V
1
2
3
4
5
6
7
8
9
10
11
12
13
14
15
16
19
Wells-next-the-Sea
Blakeney
Cley next the Sea
Sheringham
West Runton
East Runton
Cromer
Overstrand
Mundesley
Holt
Fakenham
North Walsham
Happisburgh
Aylsham
Dereham
Taverham
Drayton
Hellesdon
NORWICH
Wroxham
Hoveton
Acle
Caister-on-Sea
GREAT YARMOUTH
Gorleston-on-Sea
Hemsby
THE BROADS
Brundall
Hethersett
Wymondham
Watton
Attleborough
Loddon
Belton
LOWESTOFT
Kessingland
Beccles
Bungay
Harleston
Diss
Halesworth
Southwold
Walberswick
Dunwich
Saxmundham
Leiston
Aldeburgh
Thorpeness
Stowmarket
Needham Market
Eye
Framlingham
Wickham Market
Debenham
Mendlesham
A47
A11
A140
A143
A146
A148
A149
A12
A14
A1066
A1120
A1065
A1067
A1075
A134
A144
A145
A1094
A1095

CAERNARFON
BAY
Holyhead Bay
HOLY ISLAND
Holyhead
(Caergybi)
CARMEL HEAD
The Skerries
Dublin
Dublin (Mar-Oct)
North Stack
South Stack
Penrhyn Mawr
Trearddur Bay
Rhoscolyn
Rhoscolyn Head
Rhosneigr
Cymyran Bay
Valley
Four Mile Bridge
Llanfair-yn-Neubwll
Caergeiliog
Llanfihangel yn Nhowyn
Porth Trecastell
Aberffraw
Aberffraw Bay
Malltraeth Bay
Llanddwyn Island
Newborough
ANGLESEY
Amlwch
Point Lynas
Llaneilian
Cemaes
Cemaes Bay
Wylfa Head
Tregele
Burwen
Llanfechell
Bodewryd
Penysarn
Nebo
Llanfairynghornwy
Llanrhyddlad
Llanfaethlu
Church Bay
Carreglefn
Rhosybol
Capel Parc
Llyn Alaw
Dulas Bay
Moelfre
Llanallgo
Llanddeusant
Elim
Llanerchymedd
Llanfwrog
Llanfachraeth
Llanynghenedl
Bodedern
Capel Coch
Brynteg
Benllech
Red Wharf Bay
Llanbedrgoch
Llanddyfnan
Pentraeth
Llanddona
Puffin Island
Black Point
Llangoed
Beaumaris
Llansadwrn
Llandegfan
Menai Bridge
(Porthaethwy)
Bangor
Llynfaes
Bodffordd
Gwalchmai
Rhosmeirch
Talwrn
Llangefni
Bryngwran
Llanfaelog
Pencarnisiog
Bethel
Llangristiolus
Pentre Berw
Gaerwen
Penmynydd
Llanfairpwllgwyngyll
Llangadwaladr
Malltraeth
Llanddaniel Fab
Llangaffo
Brynsiencyn
Dwyran
Y Felinheli
Caernarfon
Abermenai Point
Llanddwyn Bay
Foryd Bay
Bontnewydd
Caeathro
Cwm-y-glo
Llanrug
Llanberis
Deiniolen
Dinorwig
Bethesda
Tregarth
Rhiwlas
Llandygai
Llanllechid
Rachub
Abergwyngregyn
Llanfairfechan
Penmaenmawr
Conwy
Conwy Bay
Llandudno
Deganwy
Great Orme
GREAT ORME'S HEAD
Dwygyfylchi
Capelulo
Henryd
Rowen
Ty'n-y-Groes
Tal-y-Bont
Dolgarrog
Vale of Conwy
ERYRI (SNOWDONIA)
NATIONAL PARK
Llanbedr-y-Cennin
Capel Curig
Nant Peris
Pass of Llanberis
Llyn Ogwen
Llyn Padarn
Waunfawr
Rhostryfan
Llanwnda
Llandwrog
Groeslon
Carmel
Penygroes
Talysarn
Pontllyfni
Llanllyfni
Nebo
Nasareth
Clynnog Fawr
Pant Glas
Bryncir
Rhyd-Ddu
Llyn Cwellyn
Beddgelert
Nantmor
Croesor
Garndolbenmaen
Dolbenmaen
Golan
Prenteg
Garreg
Tremadog
Porthmadog
Penrhyndeudraeth
Minffordd
Maentwrog
Gellilydan
Blaenau Ffestiniog
Llan Ffestiniog
Rhyd
Dolwyddelan
Betws-y-Coed
Gwydyr Forest
Pont-y-pant
Trawsfynydd
Llyn Trawsfynydd Reservoir
Borth-y-Gest
Traeth Bach
Talsarnau
Ynys
Harlech Point
Harlech
Tremadog Bay
Llanfair
Llandanwg
Llanbedr
Shell Island
Dyffryn Ardudwy
Llanddwywe
Talybont
Barmouth
Barmouth Bay
Fairbourne
Penmaenpool
Llanelltyd
Dolgellau
Brithdir
Ganllwyd
Llanfachreth
Coed-y-Brenin Forest Park
RHINOG FAWR
CADER IDRIS
Tal-y-llyn
LLYN
PENINSULA
Trefor
Llanaelhaearn
Trwyn y Gorlech
Llithfaen
Pistyll
Carreg Ddu
Morfa Nefyn
Nefyn
Porth Nefyn
Edern
Boduan
Llannor
Y Ffôr
Llangybi
Llanystumdwy
Chwilog
Criccieth
Pentrefelin
Aberech
Efailnewydd
Pwllheli
Pen-ychain
Penrhos
Llanbedrog
Trwyn Llanbedrog
St Tudwal's Road
Abersoch
Machroes
St Tudwal's Island East
St Tudwal's Island West
Porth Ceiriad
Bwlchtocyn
Llanengan
Llangian
Porth Neigwl or Hell's Mouth
Botwnnog
Sarn Mellteyrn
Bryncroes
Llaniestyn
Dinas
Tudweiliog
Porth Ysgaden
Porth Colmon
Pen-y-graig
Llangwnnadl
Porth Oer
Rhoshirwaun
Y Rhiw
Aberdaron
Aberdaron Bay
Porth Ysgo
Llanfaelrhys
Bardsey Sound
BARDSEY ISLAND
20
0 1 2 3 4 miles
0 1 2 3 4 5 kilometres

LIVERPOOL BAY
Dublin
Douglas
Belfast
Formby
Maghull
Skelmersdale
KIRKBY
CROSBY
BOOTLE
WALLASEY
LIVERPOOL
ST HELENS
Rainford
Knowsley
Prescot
Halewood
RUNCORN
BIRKENHEAD
Hoylake
West Kirby
WIRRAL
Heswall
Bebington
ELLESMERE PORT
Elton
Helsby
Neston
Point of Ayr
River Dee
River Mersey
Prestatyn
Rhyl
Rhôs-on-Sea
Colwyn Bay
(Bae Colwyn)
Abergele
Rhuddlan
St Asaph
Holywell
(Treffynnon)
Flint
(Y Fflint)
Connah's Quay
Queensferry
CHESTER
Northop
Buckley
(Bwcle)
Ewloe
Mold
(Yr Wyddgrug)
Denbigh
(Dinbych)
Ruthin
(Rhuthun)
Clwydian Range
Vale of Clwyd
Mynydd Hiraethog
Clocaenog Forest
Llandegla
Wrexham
(Wrecsam)
Gresford
Rhosllanerchrugog
Ruabon
Llangollen
Chirk
Corwen
Llantysilio Mountain
Ruabon Mountain
Cyrn-y-Brain
Berwyn
Bala
Llyn Tegid
Lake Vyrnwy
Oswestry
Ellesmere
Whittington
Llanfyllin
Welshpool
SHREWSBURY
Dinas-Mawddwy
Mallwyd
Minllyn
30
22
21
L
M
N
P
Q
R
S
T
U
V

Cleveleys
Thornton
35
Poulton-le-Fylde
BLACKPOOL
Kirkham
Lytham St Annes
Freckleton
Warton
PRESTON
BLACKBURN
Longridge
Bamber Bridge
Leyland
Darwen
Chorley
Tarleton
Longton
Eccleston
SOUTHPORT
Burscough
Ormskirk
Formby
Skelmersdale
Up Holland
WIGAN
Standish
Horwich
Adlington
Coppull
Westhoughton
Hindley
Atherton
Tyldesley
Leigh
Ince-in-Makerfield
Orrell
Abram
Ashton-in-Makerfield
Golborne
Rainford
Billinge
Maghull
KIRKBY
CROSBY
BOOTLE
LIVERPOOL
LIVERPOOL BAY
WALLASEY
BIRKENHEAD
Hoylake
West Kirby
WIRRAL
Heswall
Bebington
Knowsley
ST HELENS
Prescot
Haydock
Newton-le-Willows
Burtonwood
WARRINGTON
Halewood
WIDNES
RUNCORN
River Mersey
River Dee
ELLESMERE PORT
Neston
Frodsham
Helsby
Northwich
Cuddington
Winsford
CHESTER
Connah's Quay
Queensferry
Flint (Y Fflint)
Holywell (Treffynnon)
Prestatyn
Rhuddlan
St Asaph
Denbigh (Dinbych)
Ruthin (Rhuthun)
Mold (Yr Wyddgrug)
Buckley (Bwcle)
Wrexham (Wrecsam)
Gresford
Tarporley
Dublin
Douglas
Belfast
29
22

31
35
36
32
23
Clitheroe
Colne
Nelson
KEIGHLEY
Keighley Moor
Haworth
Bingley
Guiseley
Yeadon
Horsforth
LEEDS
Shipley
BRADFORD
Pudsey
Farsley
Cullingworth
Wilsden
Thornton
Queensbury
The Forest of Trawden
BURNLEY
Padiham
Whalley
Clayton-le-Moors
Accrington
Oswaldtwistle
Haslingden
Rawtenstall
Bacup
Todmorden
Hebden Bridge
HALIFAX
Sowerby Bridge
Brighouse
Elland
HUDDERSFIELD
Cleckheaton
Heckmondwike
Batley
Dewsbury
Mirfield
Morley
Rothwell
WAKEFIELD
Normanton
Ossett
Horbury
Littleborough
Ramsbottom
ROCHDALE
BURY
Heywood
Milnrow
Shaw
Royton
BOLTON
Radcliffe
Whitefield
Middleton
Chadderton
OLDHAM
Walkden
Prestwich
Swinton
Failsworth
Ashton-under-Lyne
Stalybridge
MANCHESTER
SALFORD
Eccles
Droylsden
Audenshaw
Dukinfield
Denton
Hyde
Stretford
Urmston
Sale
Partington
Altrincham
STOCKPORT
Cheadle
Gatley
Hale
Bowdon
Bramhall
Marple
Hazel Grove
Romiley
Glossop
Hadfield
Mossley
Meltham
Holmfirth
Penistone
Stocksbridge
BARNSLEY
Royston
Wombwell
Hoyland
Chapeltown
SHEFFIELD
Dronfield
CHESTERFIELD
PEAK DISTRICT NATIONAL PARK
HIGH PEAK
Howden Moors
Saddleworth Moor
Dove Stone Reservoir
Snake Pass
Kinder Scout
Edale
Hathersage
Bamford
Castleton
Hope
Chapel-en-le-Frith
New Mills
Disley
Poynton
Wilmslow
Knutsford
Macclesfield
Bollington
Buxton
Tideswell
Bakewell
Matlock
Wirksworth
Ashbourne
Leek
Congleton
Sandbach
Alsager
Kidsgrove
Biddulph
Holmes Chapel
Cheddleton
NEWCASTLE-UNDER-LYME
Hanley
Belper
Ripley
Alfreton
Clay Cross
Road closed weekends & bank holidays Easter-October

36
37
31
23
24
LEEDS
Morley
Rothwell
Garforth
Castleford
Knottingley
Pontefract
WAKEFIELD
Normanton
Ossett
Horbury
Selby
Howden
Goole
Hemsworth
South Elmsall
South Kirkby
Royston
Cudworth
BARNSLEY
Dodworth
Thurnscoe
Wombwell
Hoyland
Wath upon Dearne
Mexborough
Conisbrough
Swinton
Rawmarsh
ROTHERHAM
DONCASTER
Armthorpe
Bessacarr
New Rossington
Thorne
Hatfield
Crowle
SCUNTHORPE
Bottesford
Epworth
Askern
Stainforth
Adwick le Street
Maltby
Tickhill
Bawtry
Gainsborough
Dinnington
Retford
Worksop
SHEFFIELD
Chapeltown
Stocksbridge
Dronfield
Eckington
Killamarsh
Staveley
CHESTERFIELD
Bolsover
Shirebrook
Market Warsop
Edwinstowe
Ollerton
Clay Cross
North Wingfield
Wingerworth
Sutton-in-Ashfield
MANSFIELD
Kirkby-in-Ashfield
Alfreton
Matlock
Wirksworth
Ripley
Belper
Heanor
Eastwood
Hucknall
Arnold
Calverton
Newark-on-Trent
Southwell
Tuxford
Skellingthorpe
Saxilby
Market Weighton
SHERWOOD FOREST
M1
M18
M62
M180
A1(M)

37
25
26
Beverley
Cottingham
Hessle
KINGSTON UPON HULL
Hedon
Withernsea
Patrington
Easington
Kilnsea
SPURN HEAD
HUMBER ESTUARY
HOLDERNESS
Barton-upon-Humber
Immingham
GRIMSBY
Cleethorpes
Humberston
Waltham
New Waltham
Brigg
Caistor
Market Rasen
Louth
Mablethorpe
Sutton on Sea
Chapel St Leonards
Ingoldmells
Skegness
Alford
Spilsby
Horncastle
Woodhall Spa
Coningsby
Washingborough
Branston
Bracebridge Heath
Waddington
Ruskington
Sleaford
Wainfleet All Saints
Gibraltar Point
Rotterdam (Europoort) Zeebrugge
LINCOLNSHIRE WOLDS
0 1 2 3 4 miles
0 1 2 3 4 5 kilometres

Maryport
Dearham
Gilcrux
Tallentire
Bridekirk
Flimby
Broughton Moor
Standingstone
Dovenby
Papcastle
Great Broughton
Camerton
Seaton
Great Clifton
Workington
Moss Bay
Stainburn
Little Clifton
Brigham
Greysouthen
Eaglesfield
Cockermouth
Embleton
Deanscales
Dean
Branthwaite
Ullock
Pardshaw
Low Lorton
High Lorton
39
Harrington
Distington
Common End
Lowca
Parton
Howgate
Low Moresby
Gilgarran
Mockerkin
Lamplugh
Loweswater
Asby
Arlecdon
Rowrah
Kirkland
Whitehaven
Saltom Bay
Kells
Hensingham
Frizington
Cleator Moor
Sandwith
Mirehouse
Rottington
Bigrigg
Cleator
St Bees Head
St Bees Head Heritage Coast
St Bees
Egremont
Ennerdale Bridge
Ennerdale Water
Crummock Water
Buttermere
Thornhill
Haile
Nethertown
Beckermet
Calder Bridge
Sellafield Station
Wellington
Gosforth
Seascale
Drigg
Holmrook
Ravenglass
Santon Bridge
Nether Wasdale
Wast Water
Eskdale Green
Boot
Eskdale
Waberthwaite
Hycemoor
Selker Bay
Bootle
Whitbeck
The Green
Whicham
Silecroft
Kirksanton
Haverigg
Haverigg Point
Millom
The Hill
Lady Hall
Foxfield
Broughton-in-Furness
Grizebeck
Kirkby-in-Furness
Beck Side
Soutergate
Askam in Furness
Ireleth
Ulverston
Pennington
Swarthmoor
Lindal in Furness
Dalton-in-Furness
Little Urswick
Great Urswick
Newton
Stainton with Adgarley
Gleaston
Dendron
Leece
Barrow-in-Furness
Vickerstown
Rampside
Isle of Walney
Hilpsford Point
Sheep Island
Piel Island
Foulney Island
Piel Bar
South Walney
Bootle
Ulpha
Broughton Mills
Dunnerdale
Seathwaite
Torver
Coniston
Blawith
Lake District National Park
Cumbrian Mountains
Keswick
Portinscale
Braithwaite
Thornthwaite
Swinside
Bassenthwaite
Embleton
Grange
Rosthwaite
Seatoller
Honister Pass
High Stile
Dale Head
Glaramara
Great Gable
Scafell Pike
Scafell
Great End
Bow Fell
Pike of Blisco
Hardknott Pass
Wrynose Pass
Harter Fell
Tilberthwaite Fells
The Old Man of Coniston
Bowmanstead
Whitfell
Black Combe
Haycock
Seatallan
Pillar
Kirk Fell
Lank Rigg
Grasmoor
Skiddaw
Sunderland
High Ireby
Uldale
Blindcrake
Isle of Man
Point of Ayre
Point Cranstal
Rue Point
The Lhen
Bride
Andreas
Shellag Point
Jurby Head
Jurby
Sandygate
Ramsey Bay
St Judes
Sulby
Ramsey (Rhumsaa)
Ballaugh
Churchtown
Glen Auldyn
Orrisdale Head
Maughold
Maughold Head
Ballajora
North Barrule
Kirk Michael
Snaefell
Sulby Reservoir
The Bungalow
Slieau Lhean
Knocksharry
Beinn-y-Phott
Laxey
Dhoon Bay
Laxey Head
Laxey Bay
Colden
Slieau Ruy
Ellan Vannin
St Patrick's Isle
Peel (Purt ny-h-Inshey)
Contrary Head
Patrick
St John's
Glen Maye
Baldrine
Clay Head
Crosby
Glen Vine
Strang
Onchan
Onchan Head
Dalby
Foxdale
Union Mills
Douglas (Doolish)
Douglas Head
Niarbyl Bay
South Barrule
Cronk ny Arrey Laa
St Marks
Port Soderick
Santon Head
Fleshwick Bay
Grenaby
Bradda Head
Colby
Ballasalla
Port Erin
Castletown
Derbyhaven
Port St Mary
Calf of Man
Cregneash
Spanish Head
Scarlett Point
Castletown Bay
Dreswick Point
Caigher Point
Belfast
Heysham
Liverpool
Dublin
Manx Heritage site
miles
kilometres
Cleveleys
Rossall Point

Penrith
Appleby-in-Westmorland
Kirkby Stephen
Brough
Ambleside
Windermere
Bowness-on-Windermere
Kendal
Sedbergh
Hawes
Kirkby Lonsdale
Grange-over-Sands
Carnforth
Morecambe
Heysham
Lancaster
Bolton-le-Sands
Settle
Skipton
Barnoldswick
Clitheroe
Colne
Garstang
Preesall
Middleton-in-Teesdale
MORECAMBE BAY
YORKSHIRE DALES NATIONAL PARK
Forest of Bowland
Lune Forest
Dufton Fell
Stainmore Forest
Langstrothdale Chase
Howgill Fells
Swaledale
Wensleydale
Dentdale
Garsdale
Ullswater
Haweswater
Milburn Forest
Shap
Tebay
Orton
Crosby Ravensworth
Kirkby Thore
Temple Sowerby
Warcop
Ravenstonedale
Newbiggin-on-Lune
Staveley
Burneside
Milnthorpe
Arnside
Silverdale
Ingleton
Bentham
Clapham
Horton-in-Ribblesdale
Malham
Kettlewell
Grassington
Hellifield
Long Preston
Gisburn
Slaidburn
Dunsop Bridge
Chipping
M6
A6
A66
A65
A683
A684
A685
A591
A590
A592
A682
A59
40
36
30
31

Hartlepool
Middlesbrough
Stockton-on-Tees
Darlington
Billingham
Bishop Auckland
Shildon
Spennymoor
Crook
Ferryhill
Sedgefield
Newton Aycliffe
Barnard Castle
Richmond
Catterick Garrison
Catterick
Northallerton
Leyburn
Bedale
Thirsk
Masham
Ripon
Harrogate
Knaresborough
Wetherby
Skipton
Ilkley
Otley
Keighley
Guiseley
Tadcaster
Yarm
Stokesley
Easingwold
Sowerby
Boroughbridge
Pateley Bridge
Grassington
Middleton-in-Teesdale
Hurworth-on-Tees
Ingleby Barwick
Thornaby-on-Tees
Eston
Hartlepool Bay
Hamsterley Common
Stainmore Forest
Swaledale
Arkengarthdale
Wensleydale
Coverdale
Nidderdale
Forest Moor
Hambleton Hills
A1(M)
A66
A19
A59
A61
A65
A684
A167
A689
A688
A168
A170
A174
A172
A629
A6108
35
41
31
32

L
M
N
P
Q
R
S
T
U
V
1
2
3
4
5
6
7
8
9
10
11
12
13
14
15
16
Redcar
Marske-by-the-Sea
Saltburn-by-the-Sea
New Marske
Skelton
Brotton
Loftus
Guisborough
Staithes
Runswick
Whitby
Sandsend
Robin Hood's Bay
Ravenscar
Scalby
Scarborough
Cayton
Filey
Filey Bay
Hunmanby
Speeton
Bempton
Flamborough
FLAMBOROUGH HEAD
Sewerby
Bridlington
BRIDLINGTON BAY
Hornsea
NORTH YORK MOORS NATIONAL PARK
North Riding Forest Park
Howardian Hills
Goathland
Rosedale Abbey
Pickering
Malton
Norton-on-Derwent
Driffield
Pocklington
Market Weighton
Beverley
YORK
Strensall
Kirkbymoorside
Helmsley
Lastingham
Levisham
Thornton-le-Dale
Sledmere
Langtoft
Nafferton
Skipsea
Atwick
Seaton
Rolston
Mappleton
A171
A170
A169
A165
A64
A166
A614
A1079
A1039
A164
A1035
32
33

A
B
C
D
E
F
G
H
J
K
1
2
3
4
5
6
7
8
9
10
11
12
13
14
15
16
43
44
Maidens
Turnberry
Turnberry Bay
Kirkoswald
Souter Johnnie's Cottage
Crossraguel Abbey
Kirkmichael
Threave
Crosshill
Straiton
Roan of Craigoch
Dipple
Wallacetown
Kilgrammie
Dailly
Water of Girvan
Old Dailly
Penkill
Girvan
Woodland
Ailsa Craig
Pinminnoch
Barr
Dalquhairn
Knockeen
Balloch
River Stinchar
GREY HILL
Pinmore
Balligmorrie
Lendalfoot
Bennane Head
Colmonell
Pinwherry
River Stinchar
Muck Water
Ballantrae
Heronsford
Water of Tig
Barrhill
Duisk River
Cross Water
Lochton
Belfast
Larne
Currarie Port
BENERAIRD
CARLOCK HILL
ALTIMEG HILL
Glen App
Milleur Point
Corsewall Point
Lady Bay
Barnhills
Portencalzie
Kirkcolm
Loch Connell
Ervie
Low Barbeth
Cairnryan
Penwhirn Reservoir
Glenwhilly
Braid Fell
Low Salchrie
Leswalt
Knocknain
Loch Ryan
Innermessan
Castle of St John
Stranraer
Balgracie
Auchnotteroch
Black Loch
White Loch
Castle Kennedy
Chlenry
Aird
Portslogan
Broadsea Bay
Lochans
CAIRN PAT
Black Head
Portpatrick
Kildrochet House
Stoneykirk
North Milmain
Sandhead
Luce Sands
Cairngarroch
Money Head
Kirkmadrine Stones
High Ardwell
Ardwell Bay
Ardwell
Chapel Rossan
Drumbreddon
Logan
Balgowan
Port Logan Bay
Port Logan
Garrochtrie
Clanyard Bay
Kilstay
Drummore
Laggantalluch Head
Kirkmaiden
Barncorkie
Damnaglaur
High Drummore
Cailiness Point
Maryport
Cardryne
Cardrain
West Cairngaan
MULL OF GALLOWAY
THE RHINNS OF GALLOWAY
LUCE BAY
New Luce
CRAIG FELL
Glenwhan
Dunragit
Glenluce Abbey
Glenluce
Whitecrook
Ringdoo Point
Milton
Stairhaven
Auchenmalg
Mull of Sinniness
Auchenmalg Bay
Chapel Finian (ruin)
Culshabbin
Elrig
Mochrum
Mochrum Loch
Castle Loch
Whitefield Loch
Dernaglar Loch
Craighlaw
Kirkcowan
Shennanton
Loch Ronald
Barfad
CULVENNAN FELL
Carseriggan
URRALL FELL
ARTFIELD FELL
BENBRAKE HILL
Southern Upland Way
Laggangairn Standing Stones
Loch Maberry
Drumlamford
Loch Dornal
Loch Ochiltree
Knowe
Creebank
Glentrool
Bargrennan
Wood of Cree
Challoch
Minnigaff
Newton Stewart
Creebridge
Kirroughtree
Palnure
Baltersan
Causeway End
Clugston
Fell Loch
Torhouse Stone Circle
Wigtown
Bladnoch
Kirwaugh
THE MACHARS
Braehead
Kirkinner
Orchardton Bay
Barrachan
Whauphill
Little Airies
Sorbie
Druchtag Motte
Drumtroddan Cup & Ring
Drumtroddan Standing Stones
Drummoddie
Big Balcraig
'Wren's Egg' Standing Stones
Monreith
Port William
Barsalloch Fort
Barsalloch Point
Point of Leg
Broughton Mains
Pouton
Garlieston
Galloway House
Cruggleton Bay
Priory
Whithorn Story
Whithorn
Rispain Camp
St Ninian's Cave
Kidsdale
Portyerrock
Isle of Whithorn
St Ninian's Chapel (ruin)
Cutcloy
BURROW HEAD
Culscadden
Wigtown Bay
CARRICK
Galloway Forest Park
GALLOWAY
Lintern Loch
Tallaminnock
GARLEFFIN FELL
Loch Bradan
Loch Finlas
Loch Doon
Loch Doon Castle
CRAIGLEE
Carrick Forest Drive
Loch Riecawr
Loch Macaterick
SHALLOCH ON MINNOCH
POLMADDIE HILL
KIRRIEREOCH HILL
MERRICK
Loch Moan
GARWALL HILL
Loch Enoch
Loch Neldricken
Silver Flowe
Glen Trool Lodge
Bruce
Loch Trool
Loch Dee
LAMACHAN HILL
LARG HILL
MILLFORE
Clatteringshaws Loch
Bruce's Stone
Clatteringshaws
Galloway Deer Range
Wild Goat Park
Murray's
GARLICK HILL
ROUND FELL
FELL OF FLEET
Loch Grannoch
Loch Fleet
CAIRNSMORE OF FLEET
Big Water of Fleet
Cairnsmore of Fleet
Gem Rock
Creetown
Kirkmabreck
CAIRNHARROW
Cairnholy Chambered Cairns
Carsluith
Carsluith Castle
Ravenshall Point
Mossyard
Fleet Bay
Upper Ruscoe
Fleet Valley
Anworth
Cardoness Castle
Margrie
Islands of Fleet
Kirkandrews
Lennox Plunton
Girthon
Borness
Ringdoo Point
KEIRS HILL
Burnton
High Pennyvenie
Dalmellington
BENBEOCH
ENOCH HILL
Mossdale
MARATZ HILL
Ness Glen
Carsphairn Forest
Bow Burn
CAIRNSMORE OF CARSPHAIRN
Drumjohn
Carsphairn
Kendoon Loch
Garryhorn Burn
MEAUL
CORSERINE
Polmaddy Burn
MILFIRE
Loch Dungeon
Knocksheen
Garroch
BENNAN
The Glenkens
Raiders' Road Forest Drive
Black Water of Dee
AUCHENCLOY
Carstramon Wood
WHITE TOP OF CULREOCH
Scottish Industrial
A77
A714
A75
A747
A746
A716
A751
A718
A713
A712
B741
B7023
B7045
B7035
B734
B7027
B7084
B7077
B7042
B7065
B7041
B7043
B738
B798
B7005
B7052
B7085
B7004
B7021
B7063
B733
B735
B7079
0 1 2 3 4 miles
0 1 2 3 4 5 kilometres

44
45
40
34
SOLWAY FIRTH
Lowther Hills
Forest of Ae
Moffat
Beattock
Lochmaben
Lockerbie
Lochwood
Newton Wamphray
Johnstonebridge
Templand
Dinwoodie
Boreland
Corrie
Eskdalemuir
Davington
Johnstone
Samye Ling Monastery
Sandyford
Castle O'er
Bankshill
Tundergarth
Waterbeck
Middlebie
Eaglesfield
Ecclefechan
Hoddom Cross
Hoddom Mains
Kirtlebridge
Kirkpatrick-Fleming
Chapelknowe
Brydekirk
Annan
Gretna Green
Gretna
Eastriggs
Dornock
Powfoot
Cummertrees
Ruthwell
Clarencefield
Carrutherstown
Dalton
Kelhead
Mouswald
Collin
Torthorwald
Roucan
Locharbriggs
Amisfield
Tinwald
Kirkton
Holywood
Newbridge
Dumfries
Lincluden
Maxwelltown
Cargenbridge
Islesteps
Kingholm Quay
Kelton
Conheath
Glencaple
Bankend
Caerlaverock
Blackshaw
Shearington
Mabie Forest
Lochfoot
Crocketford
Beeswing
Kirkgunzeon
Kinharvie
New Abbey
Kirkconnell
Ingleston
Drumburn
Carsethorn
Kirkbean
Borron Point
Arbigland
John Paul Jones Cottage
Southerness
Southerness Point
Mainsriddle
Loaningfoot
Caulkerbush
Fairgirth
Sandyhills
Colvend
Portling
Rockcliffe
Kippford/Scaur
Palnackie
Barnbarroch
Dalbeattie
Edingham
Redcastle
Haugh of Urr
Hardgate
Springholm
Milton
Kirkpatrick Durham
Old Bridge of Urr
Crossmichael
Clarebrand
Castle Douglas
Gelston
Rhonehouse
Bridge of Dee
Laurieston
Ringford
Tongland
Twynholm
Kirkcudbright
Mutehill
Dundrennan
Auchencairn
Balcary Point
Hestan Island
Castlehill Point
Little Ross
Ross
Borgue
Kirkchrist
Loch Ken
Balmaclellan
Corsock
St John's Town of Dalry
Bogue
Moniaive
Kirkland
Tynron
Penpont
Burnhead
Thornhill
Carronbridge
Closeburn
Kirkpatrick
Auldgirth
Dalswinton
Dunscore
Stepford
Shawhead
Nithsdale
Keir Hills
Durisdeer
Enterkinfoot
Polgown
Benbuie
Corlae
Balmaclellan
Bowness-on-Solway
Port Carlisle
Glasson
Drumburgh
Cardurnock
Anthorn
Kirkbride
Moricambe Bay
Skinburness
Silloth
Seaville
Newton Arlosh
Abbeytown
Beckfoot
Holme St Cuthbert
Mawbray
Newtown
Dubmill Point
Allonby
Allonby Bay
Wigton
Waverton
Bromfield
Langrigg
Westnewton
Aspatria
Hayton
Prospect
Oughterside
Crosscanonby
Crosby
Maryport
Dearham
Gilcrux
Plumbland
Bothel
Ireby
Uldale
Torpenhow
Blennerhasset
Fletchertown
Bolton Low Houses
Boltongate
Sunderland
Bassenthwaite
Tallentire
Bridekirk
Blindcrake
Flimby
Broughton Moor
Great Broughton
Dovenby
Papcastle
Cockermouth
Embleton
Brigham
Greysouthen
Eaglesfield
Seaton
Great Clifton
Little Clifton
Stainburn
Workington
Harrington
Distington
Deanscales
Branthwaite
Dean
Low Lorton
High Lorton
Pardshaw
Ullock
Mockerkin
Loweswater
Lamplugh
Gilgarran
Common End
Lowca
Parton
Whitehaven
Moresby
Arlecdon
Asby
Rowrah
Kirkland
Frizington
Cleator Moor
Cleator
Ennerdale Bridge
Ennerdale Water
Crummock Water
Buttermere
Sandwith
St Bees Head
St Bees
Bigrigg
Egremont
Thornthwaite
Braithwaite
Portinscale
Keswick
Great Crosthwaite
Derwent Water
Grange
Rosthwaite
Seatoller
Borrowdale
Whinlatter Pass
Honister Pass
Mirehouse
Dumfries and Galloway
LAKE DISTRICT
A74(M)
A75
A76
A701
A702
A709
A710
A711
A712
A713
A762
A745
A780
A595
A596
A66
A591
A5086

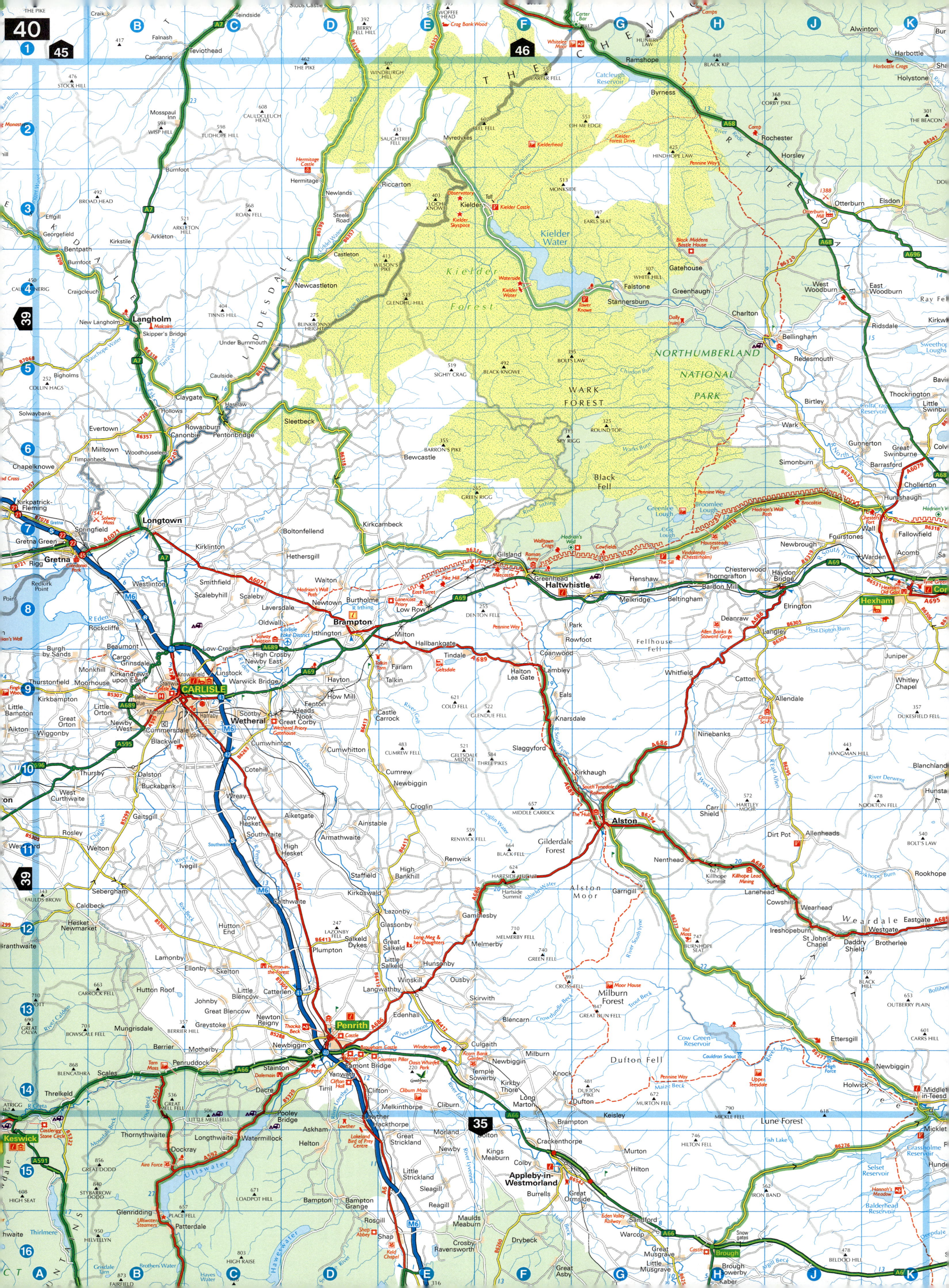
45
46
39
35
THE CHEVIOT
Carter Bar
Byrness
Rochester
Horsley
Otterburn
Elsdon
Alwinton
Harbottle
Holystone
Kielder
Kielder Water
Kielder Forest
Kielder Castle
Falstone
Stannersburn
Greenhaugh
Gatehouse
Charlton
Bellingham
Redesmouth
NORTHUMBERLAND NATIONAL PARK
WARK FOREST
Wark
Birtley
Simonburn
Gunnerton
Barrasford
Chollerton
Humshaugh
Fourstones
Newbrough
Haydon Bridge
Hexham
Bardon Mill
Henshaw
Haltwhistle
Greenhead
Gilsland
Melkridge
Beltingham
Langley
Allendale
Catton
Whitfield
Ninebanks
Alston
Nenthead
Garrigill
Kirkhaugh
Slaggyford
Knarsdale
Lambley
Coanwood
Halton Lea Gate
Tindale
Hallbankgate
Brampton
Milton
Irthington
Low Row
Burtholme
Walton
Newtown
Laverdale
Scaleby
Smithfield
Kirklinton
Hethersgill
Boltonfellend
Kirkcambeck
Bewcastle
Longtown
Gretna
Gretna Green
Springfield
Kirkpatrick-Fleming
Westlinton
Rockcliffe
CARLISLE
Wetheral
Great Corby
Scotby
Warwick Bridge
Low Crosby
High Crosby
Linstock
Cumwhinton
Cotehill
Wreay
Dalston
Thursby
Wigton
Carr Shield
Allenheads
Rookhope
Wearhead
Cowshill
Lanehead
Westgate
Eastgate
Weardale
Ireshopeburn
St John's Chapel
Daddry Shield
Brotherlee
Newcastleton
Liddesdale
Castleton
Riccarton
Steele Road
Newlands
Hermitage
Langholm
Canonbie
Rowanburn
Penton Bridge
Claygate
Harelaw
Bentpath
Burnfoot
Arkleton
Kirkstile
Teviothead
Caerlanrig
Falnash
Craik
Penrith
Stainton
Eamont Bridge
Yanwath
Clifton
Tirril
Dacre
Pooley Bridge
Askham
Helton
Hackthorpe
Great Strickland
Morland
Newby
Kings Meaburn
Bolton
Colby
Appleby-in-Westmorland
Burrells
Great Ormside
Crackenthorpe
Brampton
Murton
Hilton
Dufton
Knock
Long Marton
Kirkby Thore
Temple Sowerby
Culgaith
Langwathby
Edenhall
Melmerby
Ousby
Skirwith
Blencarn
Milburn
Hunsonby
Little Salkeld
Great Salkeld
Lazonby
Kirkoswald
Glassonby
Gamblesby
Renwick
Croglin
Armathwaite
Ainstable
Plumpton
High Hesket
Low Hesket
Southwaite
Calthwaite
Skelton
Hutton End
Ivegill
Sebergham
Caldbeck
Hesket Newmarket
Greystoke
Johnby
Little Blencow
Great Blencow
Catterlen
Newton Reigny
Motherby
Penruddock
Berrier
Mungrisdale
Threlkeld
Scales
Keswick
Thornthwaite
Dockray
Watermillock
Ullswater
Glenridding
Patterdale
Bampton
Bampton Grange
Rosgill
Shap
Sleagill
Reagill
Little Strickland
Maulds Meaburn
Crosby Ravensworth
Drybeck
Warcop
Sandford
Great Musgrave
Little Musgrave
Brough
Brough Sowerby
Kaber
Great Asby
Dufton Fell
Milburn Forest
Alston Moor
Gilderdale Forest
Lune Forest
Middleton-in-Teesdale
Mickleton
Holwick
Newbiggin
Ettersgill
Cow Green Reservoir
Hexham
Brough

47
Amble
Coquet Island
Warkworth
Rothbury
Shilbottle
Edlingham
Longframlington
Acklington
Togston
High Hauxley
Broomhill
Felton
Druridge Bay
North Northumberland Heritage Coast
Widdrington
Cresswell
Stobswood
Longhorsley
Causey Park Bridge
Ulgham
Ellington
Lynemouth
Fontburn Reservoir
Netherwitton
Longwitton
Stanton
Woodhorn
Beacon Point
Ashington
Newbiggin-by-the-Sea
Pegswood
Morpeth
Mitford
Cambo
Hartburn
Bothal
Hepscott
Middleton
Meldon
Bedlington
Blyth
Whalton
Capheaton
Belsay
Ogle
Stannington
Cramlington
Seaton Delaval
Seaton Sluice
St Mary's
Kirkheaton
Ingoe
Milbourne
Ponteland
Darras Hall
Dinnington
Whitley Bay
Tynemouth
Amsterdam (Ijmuiden)
Matfen
Longbenton
North Shields
SOUTH SHIELDS
Gosforth
Wallsend
Jarrow
Hebburn
NEWCASTLE UPON TYNE
GATESHEAD
Heddon-on-the-Wall
Ryton
Blaydon
Prudhoe
Ovingham
Wylam
Whickham
Felling
Whitburn
Marsden Bay
Stocksfield
Riding Mill
Rowlands Gill
Burnopfield
WASHINGTON
SUNDERLAND
Birtley
Stanley
Pelton
Chester-le-Street
Consett
Annfield Plain
Houghton-le-Spring
Seaham
Hetton-le-Hole
Murton
Lanchester
Sacriston
Durham
Easington Colliery
Easington
Haswell
Shotton Colliery
Peterlee
Brandon
Wheatley Hill
Wingate
Blackhall Colliery
Durham Heritage Coast
Stanhope
Frosterley
Wolsingham
Tow Law
Crook
Willington
Spennymoor
Ferryhill
Cornforth
Trimdon
Sedgefield
HARTLEPOOL
Hartlepool Bay
Bishop Auckland
Shildon
Hamsterley Common
Tees Bay
Billingham
Redcar
Marske-by-the-Sea
Newton Aycliffe
Eggleston
STOCKTON ON-TEES
MIDDLESBROUGH
Eston
Thornaby-on-Tees
Guisborough
Barnard Castle
DARLINGTON
Ingleby Barwick
Yarm
Middleton St George
Piercebridge
Gainford
Staindrop
36

48
COLONSAY
Kiloran
Kilchattan
Scalasaig
Machrins
Garvard
Oronsay
Rubha Bàn
Dubh Eilean
ORONSAY
Eilean Ghaoideamal
JURA
Glendebadel Bay
364 BEN GARRISDALE
CRUACH NA SEILCHEIG
Corpach Bay
466 BEINN BHREAC
Glen Grundale
Shian Bay
453 RAINBERG MÒR
Ardlussa
Lussa Point
Lussagiven
Loch Righ Mòr
Rubh' an t-Sàilein
Loch Tarbert
Colonsay - Port Askaig
Rubha-a' Mhàil
Rubha Bholsa
363 SGARBH BREAC
506 SCRINADLE
398 BEINN TARSUINN
Jura Forest
784 BEINN AN OIR
734
Paps of Jura
Loch Chnuic Bhric
Knockrome
Ardfernal
Jura
560 GLAS BHEINN
Feolin Ferry
Keils
Craighouse
529 DUBH BHEINN
Small Isles
342 BRAT BHEINN
Rubha na Caillich
Cabrach
Am Fraoch Eilean
Brosdale Island
Rubha na Tràille
McArthur's Head
Nave Island
Ardnave Point
Gortantaoid Point
Bunnahabhain
316 GUIR-BHEINN
Port Askaig
Keills
Finlaggan
Loch Finlaggan
Ton Mhòr
Eilean Mòr
Sanaigmore
Kilnave
Loch Gruinart
Rubha Lamanais
Loch Gorr
Lecht Gruinart
Saligo Bay
Loch Gorm
Gruinart
Gleann Mòr
Ballygrant
Loch Ballygrant
Loch Lossit
Coul Point
Sunderland
Kilchoman
Machir Bay
266 BEINNE DUBH
Bruichladdich
Loch Indaal
Bridgend
Gartachossan
Kilchiaran Bay
Bowmore
Islay Life
Port Charlotte
429 SGÒRR NAM FAOILEANN
471
ISLAY
RHINNS OF ISLAY
231 BEINN TART A'MHILL
490 BEINN BHEIGEIR
Lossit Bay
Nerabus
Laggan Point
River Laggan
Rubha Liath
Ardtalla
Claggain Bay
454 BEINN URARAIDH
Loch Uraraidh
Rubha na Faing
Portnahaven
Port Wemyss
Orsay
RHINNS POINT
Laggan Bay
Glenegedale
Kintour
Kildalton Cross
Ardmore Point
346 BEINN SHOLUM
Eilean a' Chùirn
Rubha Mòr
Kintra
165 MAOL BUIDHE
Port Ellen
Ardbeg
Lagavulin
Laphroaig
Rubha na Gainmhich
Texa
THE OA
Lower Killeyan
Risabus
Kinnabus
Loch Kinnabus
American
MULL OF OA
Rubha nan Leacan
Ballycastle (Apr-Sept)
Port Askaig - Kennacraig
Port Ellen - Kennacraig
A846
A847
B8016
B8017
B8018
0 1 2 3 4 miles
0 1 2 3 4 5 kilometres
Macaskin
Loch Crinan
Crinan
Kilmahumaig
Bellanoch
Argyll Beaver
Knapdale
Carsaig Bay
Tayvallich
Achnamara
Kilmichael of Inverlussa
Keills Chapel
466 CRUACH LUSACH
Loch Sween
Kilbride
Castle Sween
Danna Island
Lochead
Achahoish
St Cormac's Chapel
Kilmory Knap Chapel
Kilmory
Kilmory Bay
Ellary
Point of Knap
Loch Caolisport
Ormsary
SOUND OF JURA
Jura - Tayvallich (Apr-Sept)
Druimdrishaig
Loch nan Torran
480 DUBH CHREAG
Cretshengan
Coulaghailtro
Kilberry Sculptured Stones
Kilberry
Kilberry Head
Keppoch Point
Tiretigan
213 CRUACH AIRDE
Torinturk
Loch Stornoway
Ardpatrick
West Loch Tarbert
Kilchamaig
Portachoillan
Clachan
Ronachan Point
Ronachan
Loch Ciaran
Loch Garasdale
Kinerarach
Tarbert
GIGHA
247 CRUACH MHIC GOUGAIN
264 CNOC AN T-SAMHLAIDH
Ardminish
Achamore
Rhunahaorine Point
Rhunahaorine
Sound of Gigha
Tayinloan
Cara
354 CRUACH NAN GABHAR
A83
Muasdale
Glenacardoch Point
Belloch
Glenbarr
Carradale Village
Bridgend
Dippen
454 BEINN AN TUIRC
Torrisdale
319
Cleongart
Bellochantuy Bay
Bellochantuy
408 BÒRD MÒR
Saddell
Saddell Bay
396 SGREADAN HILL
Ugadale
Lussa Loch
KINTYRE
Glen Lussa
Kilkenzie
Peninver
Ardnacross Bay
Machrihanish Bay
Machrihanish
Kilmichael
Campbeltown
Campbeltown Loch
Drumlemble
Stewarton
Kilkerran
Kildalloig
Island Davaar
B842
B843
Earadale Point
385 THE STATE
352 BEINN GHUILEAN
Achinhoan
446 CNOC MOY
Dalsmeran
Conie Glen
Glen Kerran
Ru Stafnish
Glen Breakerie
Strone Glen
Cattadale
MULL OF KINTYRE
428 BEINN NA LICE
Carskey
Southend
Polliwilline Bay
Macharioch
Dunaverty
Carskey Bay
Sound of Sanda
Sheep Island
Sanda Island
Borgadalemore Point
Coll and Tiree
0 1 2 3 4 miles
0 1 2 3 4 5 kilometres
Eilean Mòr
Rubha Mòr
Rubha Sgor-innis
Bousd
Sorisdale
Cliad Bay
Arnabost
Grishipoll
Clabhach
Loch Cliad
Hogh Bay
Ballyhaugh
Arinagour
COLL
Bagh a' Chaisteil (Castlebay)
(Apr-Oct Weds only)
Oban
Totronald
Feall Bay
Arileod
Acha
Uig
Eilean Ornsay
Calgary Point
Crossapol Bay
Loch Breachacha
Rubha Fasachd
Gunna
Rubha Dubh
Rubha Port Bhiosd
Clachan Mor
Balephetrish Bay
Caoles
Ruaig
Hough Bay
Ballevullin
Cornaigmore
Kenovay
Gott Bay
Tiree
Kilkenneth
Scarinish
Middleton
Moss
Heylipoll
Crossapol
TIREE
Hynish Bay
Barrapoll
Balemartine
Mannal
Rinn Thorbhais
Balephuil Bay
Hynish
Skerryvore Lighthouse
Fladda
Lunga
TRESHNISH ISLES
Bac Mòr or Dutchman's Cap
Bac Beag

49
44
38
Loch Fyne
Lochgilphead
Lochgair
Ardrishaig
Tarbert
Kennacraig
Skipness
Claonaig
Glendaruel
Tighnabruaich
Kames
Portavadie
BUTE
Rothesay
Port Bannatyne
Kilchattan
Sound of Bute
Dunoon
Kilmun
Sandbank
Innellan
Toward
Gourock
GREENOCK
Port Glasgow
Helensburgh
Alexandria
Dumbarton
Kilpatrick Hills
Old Kilpatrick
Bishopton
Erskine
Renfrew
PAISLEY
Johnstone
Elderslie
Kilbarchan
Houston
Bridge of Weir
Kilmacolm
Inverkip
Wemyss Bay
Skelmorlie
Largs
Fairlie
Clyde Muirshiel Regional Park
Kilbirnie
Beith
Dalry
Lochwinnoch
Barrhead
Neilston
Stewarton
West Kilbride
Seamill
Ardrossan
Saltcoats
Stevenston
Kilwinning
Irvine
Irvine Bay
KILMARNOCK
Kilmaurs
Galston
Troon
Prestwick
Ayr
Ayr Bay
Mauchline
Maybole
Dalmellington
Turnberry
Maidens
Dunure
Millport
GREAT CUMBRAE ISLAND
Little Cumbrae Island
ARRAN
North Arran
Lochranza
Brodick
Lamlash
Holy Island
Whiting Bay
Kildonan
Lagg
Blackwaterfoot
Machrie Bay
Pirnmill
Corrie
Sannox
Pladda
FIRTH OF CLYDE
KILBRANNAN SOUND
Firth of Clyde
Loch Lomond
Loch Long
Gare Loch
Argyll Forest Park
Carrick Castle
Ardentinny
Glen Fruin
Garelochhead
Balloch

49
50
43
38
39
GLASGOW
STIRLING
GREENOCK
PAISLEY
KILMARNOCK
EAST KILBRIDE
Irvine
Ayr
CLYDEBANK
COATBRIDGE
HAMILTON
Gourock
Port Glasgow
Helensburgh
Alexandria
Dumbarton
Renton
Milngavie
Bearsden
Kirkintilloch
Cumbernauld
Kilsyth
Falkirk
Denny
Airdrie
Coatdyke
Chapelhall
Rutherglen
Cambuslang
Uddingston
Bellshill
Bothwell
Motherwell
Wishaw
Blantyre
Larkhall
Carluke
Lesmahagow
Stonehouse
Strathaven
Eaglesham
Newton Mearns
Barrhead
Neilston
Johnstone
Elderslie
Kilbarchan
Renfrew
Erskine
Bishopton
Kilmacolm
Houston
Bridge of Weir
Beith
Dalry
Kilbirnie
Largs
West Kilbride
Ardrossan
Saltcoats
Stevenston
Kilwinning
Kilmaurs
Stewarton
Galston
Newmilns
Darvel
Troon
Prestwick
Mauchline
Auchinleck
Cumnock
New Cumnock
Maybole
Dalmellington
Muirkirk
Douglas
Lennoxtown
Milton of Campsie
Moodiesburn
Old Kilpatrick
Duntocher
Clyde Muirshiel Regional Park
Kilpatrick Hills
Campsie Fells
Fintry Hills
Kilsyth Hills
Firth of Clyde
Loch Lomond
Irvine Bay
Ayr Bay
Cunninghame
Lady Isle
Horse Isle

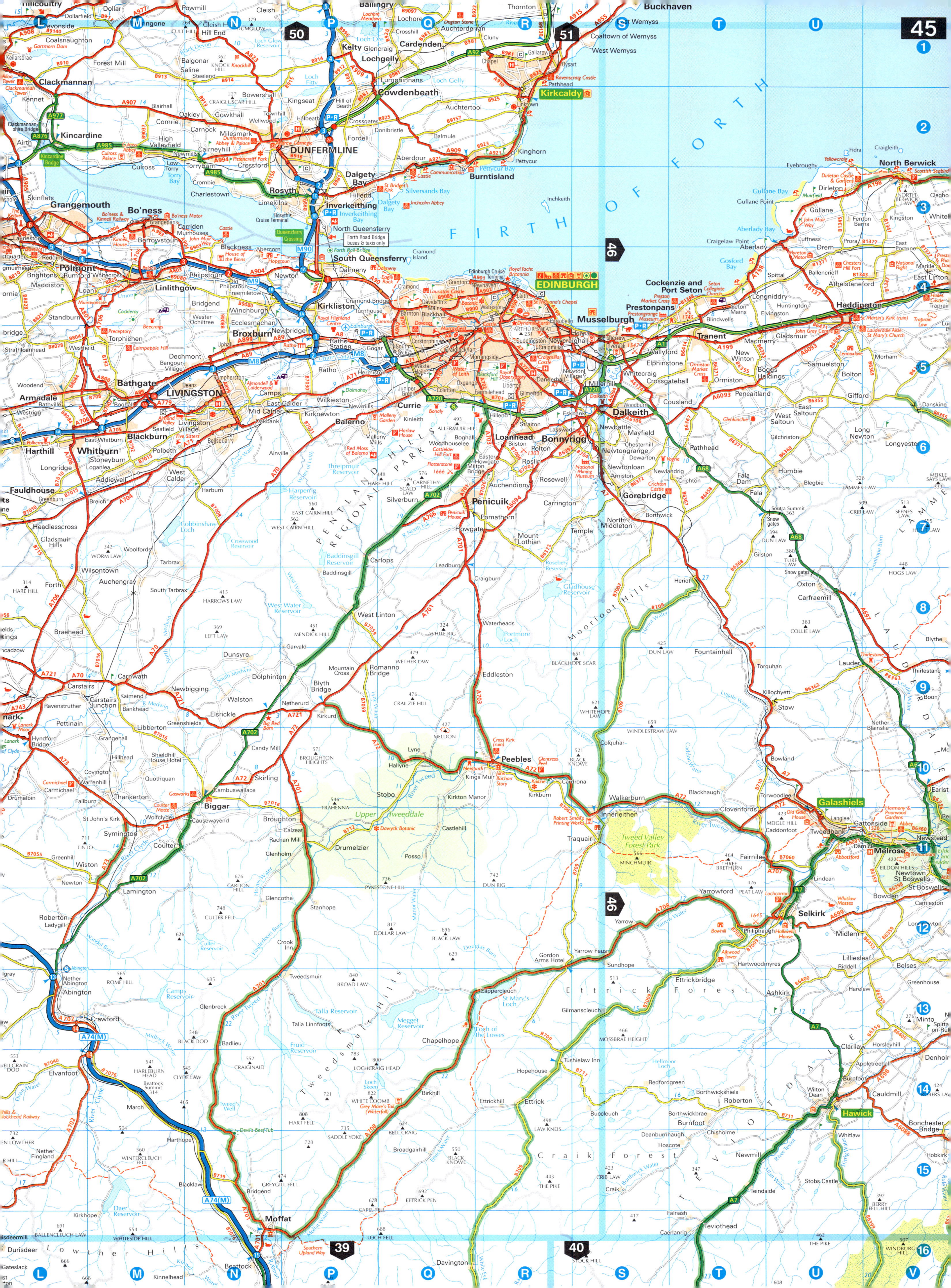
FIRTH OF FORTH
EDINBURGH
DUNFERMLINE
Kirkcaldy
Buckhaven
Wemyss
West Wemyss
Kelty
Lochgelly
Cardenden
Cowdenbeath
Burntisland
Kinghorn
Aberdour
Dalgety Bay
Inverkeithing
North Queensferry
South Queensferry
Rosyth
Limekilns
Charlestown
Crossford
Kincardine
Clackmannan
Kennet
Alloa
Culross
Grangemouth
Bo'ness
Polmont
Linlithgow
Kirkliston
Dalmeny
Broxburn
Uphall
Winchburgh
Ecclesmachan
Bathgate
LIVINGSTON
Armadale
Whitburn
Blackburn
Harthill
Fauldhouse
West Calder
Mid Calder
East Calder
Ratho
Currie
Balerno
Juniper Green
Musselburgh
Prestonpans
Cockenzie and Port Seton
Tranent
Haddington
North Berwick
Dirleton
Gullane
Aberlady
Longniddry
Dalkeith
Bonnyrigg
Loanhead
Lasswade
Penicuik
Gorebridge
Newtongrange
Mayfield
Pathhead
West Linton
Carlops
Peebles
Innerleithen
Walkerburn
Galashiels
Melrose
Selkirk
Hawick
Lauder
Stow
Biggar
Carnwath
Lanark
Carstairs
Abington
Crawford
Moffat
Broughton
Tweedsmuir
Ettrick
Yarrow
Lindean
Newstead
St Boswells
Denholm
Teviothead
PENTLAND HILLS REGIONAL PARK
Moorfoot Hills
Tweedsmuir Hills
Ettrick Forest
Craik Forest
TEVIOTDALE
LAUDERDALE
Lowther Hills
Upper Tweeddale
Tweed Valley Forest Park
River Tweed
Talla Reservoir
Megget Reservoir
Fruid Reservoir
Gladhouse Reservoir
Cobbinshaw Loch
St Mary's Loch
Loch of the Lowes
Daer Reservoir
Grey Mare's Tail
Devil's Beef Tub
A1
A7
A68
A70
A71
A72
A701
A702
A703
A707
A708
A720
A74(M)
A985
M8
M9
M90
Forth Road Bridge
Queensferry Crossing
Kincardine Bridge
Inchkeith
Cramond Island
Fidra
Craigleith

Firth of Forth
Edinburgh
Kirkcaldy
Dunfermline
Cowdenbeath
Lochgelly
Kelty
Burntisland
Inverkeithing
North Queensferry
South Queensferry
Forth Road Bridge buses & taxis only
Queensferry Crossing
Rosyth
Dalgety Bay
Musselburgh
Prestonpans
Cockenzie and Port Seton
Tranent
Haddington
North Berwick
Dunbar
Dalkeith
Bonnyrigg
Loanhead
Penicuik
Gorebridge
Currie
Balerno
Kirkliston
Peebles
Galashiels
Melrose
Selkirk
Kelso
Jedburgh
Hawick
Lauder
Earlston
Innerleithen
Moffat
Pentland Hills Regional Park
Moorfoot Hills
Lammermuir Hills
Lauderdale
Teviotdale
Ettrick Forest
Craik Forest
Tweedsmuir Hills
Upper Tweeddale
Tweed Valley Forest Park
The Cheviots
45
40

L
M
N
P
Q
R
S
T
U
V
1
2
3
4
5
6
7
8
9
10
11
12
13
14
15
16
Pease Bay
Siccar Point
Fast Castle Head
ST ABB'S HEAD
BROWN RIG
Coldingham Loch
St Abbs
Coldingham Bay
Grantshouse
Coldingham
Houndwood
Heugh Head
Cairncross
Eyemouth
HORSELEY HILL
Reston
Ayton
Burnmouth
Auchencrow
Marygold
Lintlaw
Lamberton
Preston
Chirnside
Marshall Meadows Bay
Cumledge
Edrom Church
Foulden
North Northumberland Heritage Coast
Edrom
Chirnsidebridge
Manderston
Broadhaugh
Edington
Foulden Tithe Barn
Allanton
Hutton
Whiteadder Water
Berwick-upon-Tweed
Barracks & Main Guard
Town Ramparts
Castle
Blackadder
Paxton
Tweedmouth
Whitsome
Hilton
Spittal
Sinclair's Hill
Huds Head
Horndean
Horncliffe
Scremerston
Ladykirk
Murton
Swinton
Norham
Thornton
Cheswick
Simprim
Upsettlington
Causeway flooded at high tide
Ancroft
River Tweed
Haggerston
HOLY ISLAND
Leitholm
Holy Island
Beal
Lindisfarne Castle
Lindisfarne Priory
Castle Point
Guile Point
Duddo
Bowsden
The Hirsel
Lennel
River Till
Coldstream
Cornhill-on-Tweed
Etal
Lowick
Fenwick
Heatherslaw Light Railway
Heatherslaw Corn Mill
Lady Waterford Hall
Longstone
Wark
Buckton
FARNE ISLANDS
Shidlaw
Branxton
Crookham
Staple Sound
Ford
Inner Sound
North Northumberland Heritage Coast
Budle Bay
Bamburgh
St Cuthbert's Cave
Thornington
Howtel
Fenton
Belford
Grace Darling
Milfield
Nesbit
Seahouses
Doddington
North Sunderland
Lanton
Yeavering
Coupland
Lucker
Kirknewton
YEAVERING BELL
Humbleton Hill
Akeld
Beadnell
Kirk Yetholm
Chatton
Warenford
Wooler
Ad Gefrin
Chathill
Swinhoe
Beadnell Bay
Primsidemill
Newstead
Tughall
Ellingham
Newtown
High Newton-by-the-Sea
Wild Cattle Park
Ros Castle
Preston
Preston Tower
NORTHUMBERLAND
Pennine Way
Embleton & Newton Links
PRESTON HILL
Christon Bank
THE CURR
CATERAN HILL
Embleton
Embleton Bay
North Charlton
Dunstanburgh Castle
NATIONAL
THE SCHIL
Ilderton
Old Bewick
Fallodon
South Charlton
Mowhaugh
THE CHEVIOT
Dunstan
New Bewick
Eglingham
Rock
Craster
PARK
Rennington
Stamford
Cullernose Point
DUNMOOR HILL
Beanley
Howick Hall
Howick
Linhope Spout
Branton
Powburn
Longhoughton
Ingram
Glanton
Denwick
Boulmer
WINDY GYLE HILL
CUSHAT LAW
COCHRANE PIKE
River Aln
Hulne
Bolton
Alnwick
Seaton Point
Aln Valley Railway
Lesbury
Whittingham
Alnmouth
Alnmouth Bay
SHILLHOPE LAW
Alnham
Edlingham
Shilbottle
King Charles III England Coast Path
Netherton
LONG CRAG
GLANTLEES HILL
Alwinton
Burradon
Newton-on-the-Moor
Warkworth Castle & Hermitage
Warkworth
Amble
Harbottle
Coquet Island
Harbottle Crags
Sharperton
Gloster Hill
High Hauxley
Holystone
Snitter
Guyzance
Hepple
Thropton
Rothbury
Cragside
Acklington
Togston
CORBY PIKE
Longframlington
Felton
Broomhill
41
0 1 2 3 4 miles
0 1 2 3 4 5 kilometres

59
52
42
The Small Isles
All vehicles must have the relevant island permit prior to travel to The Small Isles. Services are seasonal, day & weather dependent.
Sound of Rùm
Rubha nam Meirleach
Bay of Laig
Cleadale
Laig
EIGG
AN CRUACHAN
Rubha an Fhasaidh
Kildonnan
Galmisdale
Eilean Chathastail
AN SGÙRR
Sound of Eigg
Eilean nan Each
MUCK
Port Mòr
Arisaig
Back of Keppoch
Bunacaimb
Eilean Ighe
Loch nan Ceall
Luinga Mhòr
Rubh' Arisaig
CRUACH DOIRE
Druimindarroch
Arisaig House
Prince's Cairn
Kinlochnanuagh
Loch nan Uamh
SIDHEAN MÒR
CARN A' MHADAIDH-RUAIDH
Meoble
MEITH BHEINN
AN STAC
SGURR BREAC
Loch Beoraid
SGÙRR AN UTHA
Polnish
Lochailort
Inverailort
Loch Eilt
Glenfinnan
A830
A861
Ardnish
Loch Ailort
Sound of Arisaig
Rubha Chuaiais
Smirisary
Glenuig
ROIS-BHEINN
BEINN ODHAR BHEAG
BEINN GAIRE
Eilean Shona
Loch Moidart
Kinlochmoidart
Brunery
Ardmolich
Glen Moidart
Glen Forsain
MOIDART
Loch Shiel
Scamodale
SGOR AN TARMACHAIN
MEALL MÒR
BEINN BHREAC
Mingarrypark
Langal
Dalnabreck
Dalelia
Loch Doilet
Glen Hurich
Polloch
SGURR DHOMHNUILL
Rubha Àird Druimnich
Ockle Point
Morar, Moidart and Ardnamurchan
Ardtoe
Shielfoot
Kentra
Arevegaig
Blain
Acharacle
Sanna Point
Sanna Bay
Sanna
Portuairk
Achnaha
Kilmory
Branault
Ockle
BEINN BHREAC
MEALL NAN CON
ARDNAMURCHAN
Ardnamurchan Point
Achosnich
BEINN NA SEILG
Kilchoan
Ormsaigmore
Mingary
Loch Mudle
BEN HIANT
Natural History
Glenbeg
Glenborrodale
Ardslignish
Laga
BEN LAGA
Salen
Resipole Burn
BEINN RESIPOL
SUNART
Ariundle Oakwood
Anaheilt
Strontian
Loch Sunart
Camasine
Woodend
Ardnastang
Camasachoirce
Liddesdale
Achnalea
Glen Tarbert
GEARR CHREAG
Glencripesdale
Oronsay
Carna
Auliston Point
Bàgh a' Chaisteil (Castlebay)
Loch Baghasdail (Lochboisdale) (Oct-Mar)
Eilean Mòr
Rubha Mòr
Rubha Sgor-innis
Sorisdale
Bousd
Arinagour
COLL
Eilean Ornsay
Tiree
Ardmore Point
Sorne Point
Glengorm Castle
Quinish Point
Rubha nan Gall
Tobermory
Calve Island
Drimnin
Loch Teacuis
BEINN LADAIN
MEALL A' CHOISE
Lochuisge
GLAS BHEINN
CREACH BHEINN
Kingairloch
BEINN NA CILLE
Caliach Point
'S AIRDE BEINN
Dervaig
Achnadrish
Calgary
Art in Nature
Old Byre
Calgary Bay
Loch Frisa
SPEINNE MÒR
BEINN BHUIDHE
SITHEAN NA RAPLAICH
Loch Arienas
Glen Dubh
Acharn
Claggan
Gleann Geal
BEINN MHEADHOIN
SGURR A' BHUIC
Treshnish Point
Ensay
CARN MÒR
Larachbeg
MEALL DAMH
Rannoch River
Achranich
Loch Tearnait
Rubh' a' Chaoil
Burg
Glen Aros
Glenaros House
Aros
Sound of Mull
Fuinary
Lochaline
Loch Aline
Fladda
Fanmore
CNOC AN DA CHINN
Ballygown
Loch Tuath
Salen
Fishnish Point
Fishnish Pier
GLAS BHEINN
AN SLEAGHACH
Lunga
TRESHNISH ISLES
Gometra
ULVA
Eas Fors
Oskamull
BEINN NAN CARN
Killiechronan
Gruline
Macquarie Mausoleum
BEINN NAN LUS
Glen Forsa
ISLE OF MULL
Scallastle Bay
Altcreich
Rubha an Ridire
Bernera Island
LISMORE
Port Ramsay
Clachan
Lismore
Achnacroish
Lynn of Lorn
Loch Linnhe
Kilcheran
Bac Mòr or Dutchman's Cap
Bac Beag
Little Colonsay
Staffa
Fingal's
Loch na Keal
Inch Kenneth
Inchkenneth Chapel (ruin)
Loch na Keal Isle of Mull
Forsa
BEINN A' GHRAIG
BEINN MHEADHON
DUN DA GHAOITHE
Craignure
Duart Bay
Duart Point
Duart
Lochdonhead
Lochdon
Gorsten
Grass Point
Ardmucknish Bay
Dunstaffnage Castle & Chapel
North Connel
Dunbeg
Ganavan Bay
Dunollie
Oban War & Peace
McCaig's Tower
Oban (An t-Òban)
A85
Balnahard
BEN MORE
CRUACHAN DEARG
BEINN NA SREINE
CREACH BHEINN
Fossil Tree
Burg
Tiroran
Aird of Kinloch
Glen More
Strathcoil
CARN BAN
KERRERA
Gylen
Gallanachbeg
Gallanachmore
Ariogan
Loch Nell
Lerags
Kilmore
IONA
Iona Abbey & Nunnery
Baile Mòr
MacLean's Cross
Kintra
Fionnphort
Rubha nan Cearc
Loch Scridain
Pennycross
Pennyghael
Loch Fuaran
BEN BUIE
BEN CREACH
Loch Spelve
Croggan
Rubha Seanach
Ardentallen
St Columba Exhibition Centre
Ardalanish
Loch Assapol
Bunessan
ROSS OF MULL
CRUACHAN MIN
BEINN NA CROISE
Lochbuie
Loch Buie
Loch Uisg
MAOL BAN
DRUIM FADA
Firth of Lorne
Knipoch
Kilninver
AN CREACHAN
Loch Scammadale
Sound of Iona
Erraid
Soa Island
Uisken
Ardchiavaig
BEINN CHREAGACH
Carsaig
Rubha Dubh
Rubha nam Braithrean
Malcolm's Point
Insh Island
Clachan-Seil
SEIL
Ellenabeich
Easdale
Slate Islands
Balvicar
Ardmaddy
Loch Tralaig
Rubh' Ardalanish
Torran Rocks
Colonsay - Oban
Garbh Eileach
GARVELLACHS
Monastery & Beehive Cells
Eileach an Naoimh
Eilean Dubh Mòr
LUNGA
Scarba, Lunga and the Garvellachs
SCARBA
CRUACH SCARBA
Sound of Luing
Cullipool
Toberonochy
LUING
SHUNA
Shuna Sound
Shuna Point
Cuan
Degnish
Melfort
Kilmelford
Loch Melfort
Arduaine Garden
Arduaine
Gleann Domhain
Barrananaoil
Craobh Haven
Craigdhu
Inverliever Lodge
Kintraw
Ardfern
Ford
Gulf of Corryvreckan
Eilean Dubh
Rubh' a' Geodha
Kiloran Bay
CARNAN EOIN
COLONSAY
Kiloran
Kilchattan
Glengarrisdale Bay
CRUACH NA SEILCHEIG
Craignish Point
Island Macaskin
Aird
Loch Craignish
Carnasserie Castle
Glebe Cairn
Kilmartin
Slockavullin
Temple Wood Stone Circles
The Nether Largie Standing Stones
Dunchraigaig Cairn
Loch Leathan
Ri Cruin Cairn
0 1 2 3 4 miles
0 1 2 3 4 5 kilometres

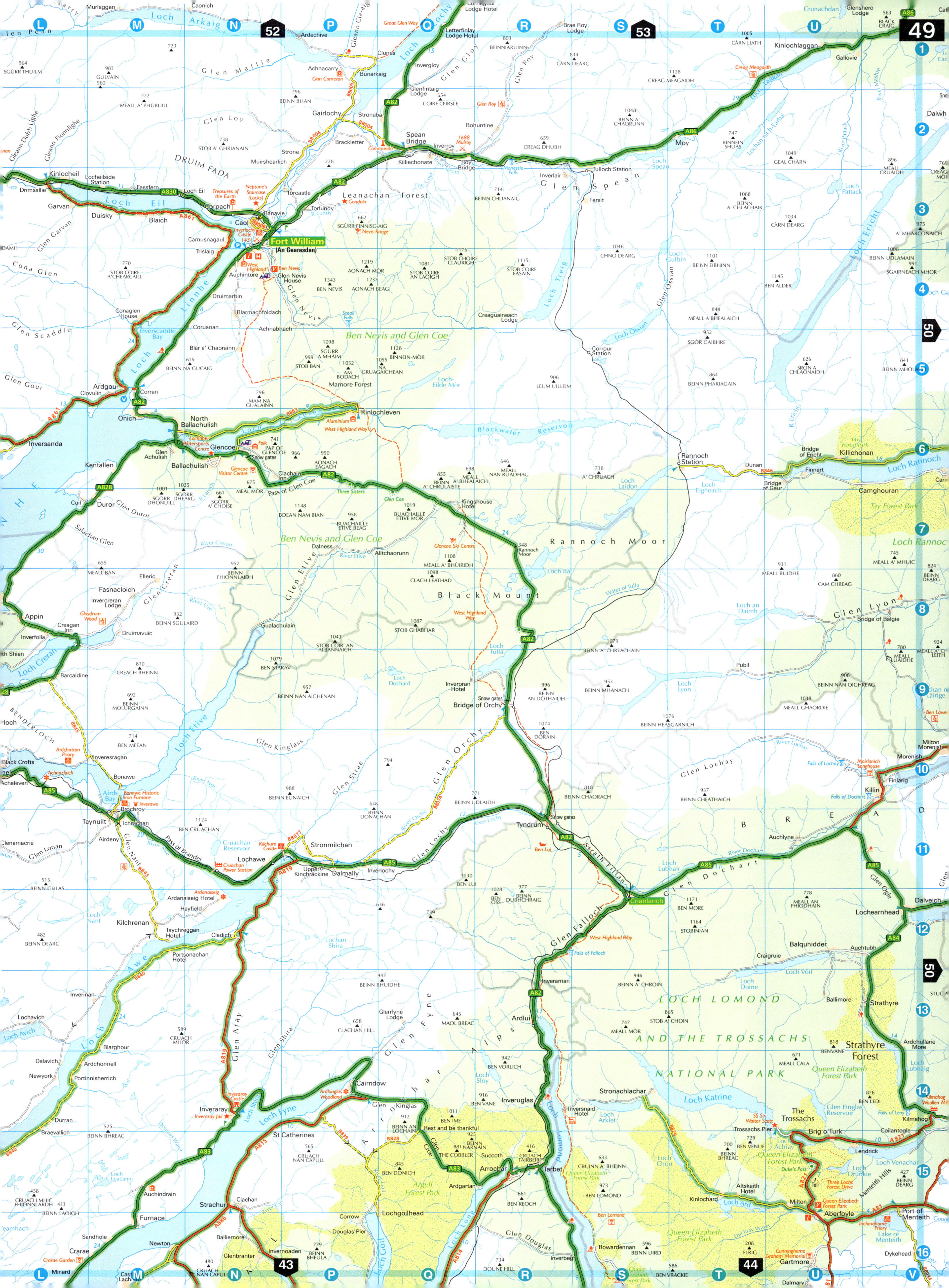

49
52
53
43
44
50
Loch Arkaig
Murlaggan
Caonich
Ardechive
Great Glen Way
Letterfinlay Lodge Hotel
Brae Roy Lodge
Kinlochlaggan
Crunachdan
Glenshero Lodge
BLACK CRAIG
Glen Mallie
GULVAIN
SGÙRR THUILM
MEALL A' PHÙBUILL
Achnacarry
Clan Cameron
Bunarkaig
Clunes
Loch Lochy
Invergloy
Glen Gloy
Glen Roy
CÀRN LIATH
CREAG MEAGAIDH
Creag Meagaidh
Gallovie
BEINN BHAN
Glenfintaig Lodge
COIRE CEIRSLE
Glen Roy
CÀRN DEARG
Gairlochy
Stronaba
Spean Bridge
Commando
Inverroy
1688 Mulroy
Bohuntine
CREAG DHUBH
BEINN A' CHAORUNN
Moy
BINNEIN SHUAS
Loch Laggan
GEAL CHÀRN
Dalwhinnie
Glen Loy
STOB A' GHRIANAIN
DRUIM FADA
Strone
Muirshearlich
Brackletter
Killiechonate
Roy Bridge
Monessie Falls
Inverlair
Tulloch Station
Glen Spean
Loch Spean
Kinlocheil
Locheilside Station
Drimsallie
Fassfern
Loch Eil
Corpach
Treasures of the Earth
Neptune's Staircase (Locks)
Torcastle
Leanachan Forest
Gondola
Fersit
Garvan
Duisky
Blaich
Caol
Banavie
Tomlundy
SGÙRR FINNISG-AIG
Nevis Range
BEINN CHLIANAIG
BEINN A' CHLACHAIR
CÀRN DEARG
Loch Pattack
Loch Ericht
A' MHARCONAICH
Glen Garvan
Camusnagaul
Inverlochy Castle
Fort William
(An Gearasdan)
Trislaig
Cona Glen
STOB COIRE A' CHEARCAILL
West Highland
Ben Nevis
Auchintore
Glen Nevis House
AONACH MÒR
AONACH BEAG
BEN NEVIS
STOB COIRE AN LAOIGH
STOB CHOIRE CLAURIGH
STOB COIRE EASAIN
CHNO DEARG
Loch Gulbin
BEINN EIBHINN
BEN ALDER
BEINN UDLAMAIN
SGAIRNEACH MHOR
Loch Linnhe
Druimarbin
Conaglen House
Blarmachfoldach
Glen Nevis
Steall Falls
Loch Treig
Creaguaineach Lodge
Glen Ossian
MEALL A' BHEALAICH
Glen Scaddle
Coruanan
Inverscaddle Bay
Achriabhach
Ben Nevis and Glen Coe
Loch Ossian
SGÒR GAIBHRE
Corrour Station
Blàr a' Chaorainn
SGÙRR A' MHÀIM
BINNEIN MÒR
STOB BAN
AM BODACH
NA GRUAGAICHEAN
Mamore Forest
Loch Eilde Mòr
BEINN NA GUCAIG
LEUM UILLEIM
BEINN PHARLAGAIN
SRON A' CHLAONAIDH
BEINN MHOLACH
Glen Gour
Ardgour
Clovulin
Corran
MAM NA GUALAINN
Kinlochleven
Aluminium
West Highland Way
Blackwater Reservoir
Onich
North Ballachulish
Loch Leven
Inversanda
Lochaber Watersports Centre
Glencoe
Folk
PAP OF GLENCOE
Snow gates
AONACH EAGACH
MEALL A' BHEALAICH
MEALL NAN RUADHAG
BEINN A' CHRULAISTE
A' CHRUACH
Loch Laidon
Rannoch Station
Dunan
Bridge of Ericht
Killichonan
Finnart
Loch Rannoch
Kentallen
Glen Achulish
Ballachulish
Glencoe Visitor Centre
Clachaig Inn
Pass of Glen Coe
Three Sisters
Glen Coe
Kingshouse Hotel
Loch Eigheach
Bridge of Gaur
Camghouran
Tay Forest Park
Duror
SGORR DHONUILL
SGORR DHEARG
SGÒRR A' CHOISE
MEAL MÒR
BIDEAN NAM BIAN
BUACHAILLE ETIVE BEAG
BUACHAILLE ETIVE MÒR
Glen Duror
Cuil
Salachan Glen
River Creran
Dalness
Glen Etive
River Etive
Alltchaorunn
Glencoe Ski Centre
Rannoch Moor
Rannoch Moor
Loch Rannoch
MEALL BÀN
BEINN FHIONNLAIDH
MEALL A' BHÙIRIDH
CLACH LEATHAD
Loch Ba
MEALL BUIDHE
CAM CHREAG
MEALL A' MHUIC
BEINN DEARG
Elleric
Fasnacloich
Glen Creran
Invercreran Lodge
Black Mount
Water of Tulla
Loch an Daimh
Glen Lyon
Appin
Glasdrum Wood
BEINN SGULAIRD
River Ure
West Highland Way
STOB GHABHAR
Bridge of Balgie
Creagan Inn
Druimavuic
Gualachulain
STOB COIR' AN ALBANNAICH
Loch Tulla
BEINN A' CHREACHAIN
Inverfolla
Loch Creran
Barcaldine
CREACH BHEINN
BEN STARAV
Loch Dochard
Inveroran Hotel
Pubil
MEALL LUAIDHE
BEINN MHANACH
Loch Lyon
BEINN NAN OIGHREAG
Benderloch
BEINN MOLURGAINN
BEINN NAN AIGHENAN
Snow gates
Bridge of Orchy
BEINN AN DOTHAIDH
MEALL GHAORDIE
Loch Etive
BEN DORAIN
BEINN HEASGARNICH
Ben Lawers
Ardchattan Priory
BEN MEEAN
Glen Kinglass
Glen Orchy
River Lochay
Milton Morenish
Inveresragan
Black Crofts
Achnacloich
Bonawe
River Noe
Glen Strae
Glen Lochay
Falls of Lochay
Moirlanich Longhouse
Morenish
Achaleven
Airds Bay
Bonawe Historic Iron Furnace
Inverawe
BEINN EUNAICH
BEINN DONACHAIN
BEINN UDLAIDH
BEINN CHAORACH
BEINN CHEATHAICH
Finlarig
Killin
Falls of Dochart
Taynuilt
Brochroy
Ichrachan
BEN CRUACHAN
Cruachan Reservoir
Kilchurn Castle
Stronmilchan
River Orchy
River Lochy
Tyndrum
Snow gates
BREADALBANE
Auchlyne
Glenamacrie
Airdeny
Glen Lonan
Glen Nant
Pass of Brander
Cruachan Power Station
Lochawe
Upper Kinchrackine
Dalmally
Inverlochy
Glen Lochy
Ben Lui
Strath Fillan
Loch Lubhair
River Dochart
Glen Dochart
Glen Ogle
BEINN GHLAS
Ardanaiseig
Ardanaiseig Hotel
Hayfield
BEN LUI
BEN OSS
BEINN DUBHCHRAIG
Crianlarich
BEN MORE
MEALL AN FHIODHAIN
Dalveich
Lochearnhead
Kilchrenan
Loch Nant
Taychreggan Hotel
Cladich
Glen Falloch
West Highland Way
STOBINIAN
Balquhidder
Auchtubh
BEINN DEARG
Loch Awe
Portsonachan Hotel
Lochan Shira
Falls of Falloch
Craigruie
Loch Voil
Inverinan
BEINN BHUIDHE
Inverarnan
BEINN A' CHROIN
Loch Doine
Ballimore
Strathyre
Lochavich
Loch Avich
Glen Aray
Glen Shira
Glenfyne Lodge
CLACHAN HILL
MAOL BREAC
Ardlui
Loch Lomond and The Trossachs National Park
STOB A' CHOIN
MEALL MÒR
BENVANE
Strathyre Forest
Ardchullarie More
Blarghour
CRUACH MHOR
Arrochar Alps
Glen Fyne
BEN VORLICH
MEALL CALA
Queen Elizabeth Forest Park
Loch Lubnaig
Dalavich
Ardchonnell
Newyork
Portinnisherrich
Loch Sloy
Cairndow
Ardkinglas Woodland
Stronachlachar
Loch Katrine
BEN LEDI
Kilmahog Woollen Mill
Inveraray
Inveraray Castle
Inveraray Jail
Loch Shira
Loch Fyne
Glen Kinglas
BEINN AN LOCHAIN
Rest and be thankful
BEN IME
BEINN NARNAIN
BEN VANE
Inveruglas
Inversnaid Hotel
Loch Arklet
SS Sir Walter Scott
Trossachs Pier
The Trossachs
Glen Finglas Reservoir
Falls of Leny
Kilmahog
Durran
Braevallich
BEINN BHREAC
St Catherines
CRUACH NAN CAPULL
Glen Croe
THE COBBLER
Succoth
CRUACH TAIRBEIRT
CRUINN A' BHEINN
BEN VENUE
BEINN BHREAC
Loch Achray
Brig o' Turk
Coilantogle
Lendrick
Loch Leacann
BEN DONICH
Argyll Forest Park
Arrochar
Tarbet
Queen Elizabeth Forest Park
Loch Chon
Queen Elizabeth Forest Park
Duke's Pass
Loch Drunkie
Loch Venachar
Menteith Hills
BEINN DEARG
Auchindrain
Ardgartan
BEN LOMOND
Kinlochard
Altskeith Hotel
Loch Ard
Three Lochs Forest Drive
Queen Elizabeth Forest Park
Toll
CRUACH MHIC FHIONNLAIDH
BEINN LOCHAIN
Strachur
Clachan
Lochgoilhead
BEN REOCH
Milton
Aberfoyle
Port of Menteith
Furnace
Corrow
Douglas Pier
Loch Long
Glen Douglas
Ben Lomond
Inchmahome Priory
Lake of Menteith
Lochawach
Sandhoie
Newton
Balliemore
Invernoaden
BEINN BHEULA
Rowardennan
BEINN UIRD
Queen Elizabeth Forest Park
Duchray Water
ELRIG
Cunninghame Graham Memorial
Gartmore
Dykehead
Crarae
Crarae Garden
Glenbranter
CRUACH NAN CAPULL
DOUNE HILL
Inverbeg
BEN VRACKIE
Dalmary
Minard
Castle Lachlan
Loch Goil
A82
A86
A830
A861
A828
A85
A819
A83
A815
A886
A84
A81
A821
A814
A846
B8004
B8005
B863
B8077
B8074
B845
B840
B828
B839
B829
L
M
N
P
Q
R
S
T
U
V
1
2
3
4
5
6
7
8
9
10
11
12
13
14
15
16

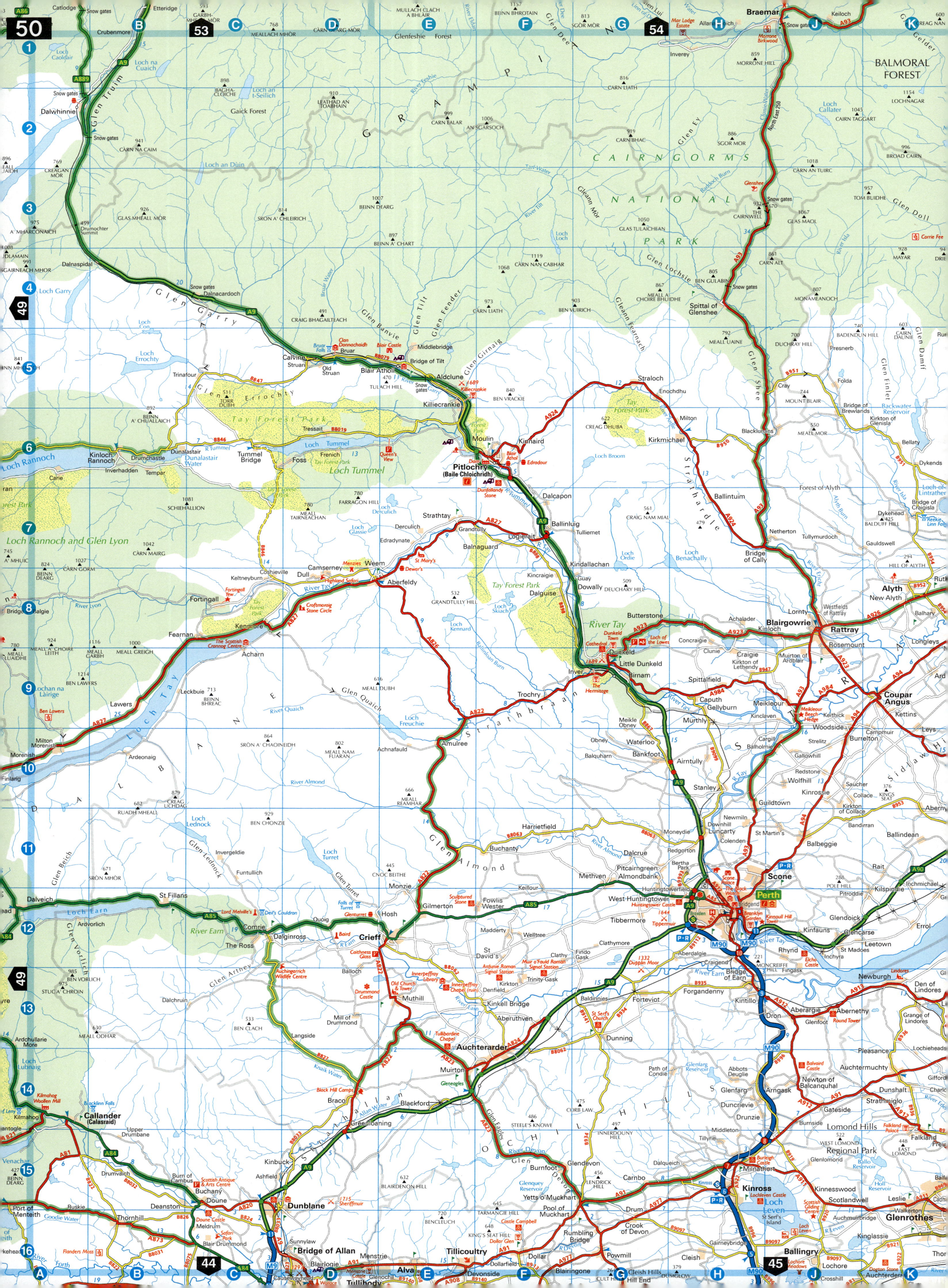

53
54
49
44
45
Braemar
Keiloch
BALMORAL FOREST
Crubenmore
Dalwhinnie
Glen Truim
Gaick Forest
Loch an Dùin
GRAMPIAN
CAIRNGORMS NATIONAL PARK
Glen Feshie
Mar Lodge Estate
Inverey
Morrone Birkwood
Loch Callater
LOCHNAGAR
CAIRN TAGGART
BROAD CAIRN
Glenshee
THE CAIRNWELL
GLAS MAOL
Spittal of Glenshee
Glen Shee
Dalnaspidal
Loch Garry
Dalnacardoch
Glen Garry
Glen Tilt
Glen Fender
Glen Banvie
Middlebridge
Bridge of Tilt
Blair Atholl
Blair Castle
Calvine
Struan
Old Struan
Bruar
Clan Donnachaidh Museum
Loch Errochty
Trinafour
Glen Errochty
Tay Forest Park
Killiecrankie
Moulin
Kinnaird
Edradour
Pitlochry (Baile Chloichridh)
Straloch
Enochdhu
Kirkmichael
Strathardle
Ballintuim
Bridge of Cally
Loch Rannoch
Kinloch Rannoch
Dunalastair
Tummel Bridge
Foss
Loch Tummel
Queen's View
Tressait
French
Loch Rannoch and Glen Lyon
Schiehallion
Strathtay
Grandtully
Logierait
Ballinluig
Tulliemet
Dalcapon
Kindallachan
Guay
Dowally
Dalguise
Aberfeldy
Weem
Menzies Castle
Dewar's
St Mary's
Camserney
Dull
Coshieville
Keltneyburn
Fortingall
Kenmore
Croftmoraig Stone Circle
The Scottish Crannog Centre
Acharn
Fearnan
Loch Tay
Lawers
Ben Lawers
Milton Morenish
Morenish
Ardeonaig
Finlarig
Butterstone
Loch of the Lowes
River Tay
Dunkeld
Dunkeld Town
Cathedral
Little Dunkeld
Birnam
Inver
The Hermitage
Trochry
Strathbraan
Amulree
Glen Quaich
Loch Freuchie
Achnafauld
River Almond
Glen Almond
Harrietfield
Buchanty
Blairgowrie
Rattray
Kinloch
Lornty
Alyth
New Alyth
Coupar Angus
Kettins
Woodside
Meikleour
Meikleour Beech Hedge
Kinclaven
Caputh
Gellyburn
Spittalfield
Murthly
Stanley
Airntully
Waterloo
Bankfoot
Obney
Meikle Obney
Luncarty
Guildtown
Balbeggie
Scone
Scone Palace
Perth
Huntingtowerfield
Almondbank
Pitcairngreen
Methven
Dalcrue
Redgorton
Bertha Park
West Huntingtower
Huntingtower Castle
Tibbermore
Kinfauns
Glencarse
St Madoes
Rhynd
Kilspindie
Rait
Errol
Newburgh
Bridge of Earn
Kintillo
Dron
Aberargie
Abernethy
Glenfoot
Forgandenny
Forteviot
Dupplin Moor
Aberdalgie
Craigend
Moncreiffe
Pleasance
Auchtermuchty
Newton of Balcanquhal
Strathmiglo
Gateside
Lomond Hills
Lomond Hills Regional Park
Falkland
Kinross
Loch Leven
Milnathort
Kinnesswood
Scotlandwell
Leslie
Glenrothes
Ballingry
Lochore
Auchterderran
Kinglassie
Cleish
Gairneybridge
Powmill
Crook of Devon
Drum
Carnbo
Rumbling Bridge
Glendevon
Yetts o' Muckhart
Pool of Muckhart
Blairingone
Dollar
Tillicoultry
Alva
Menstrie
Tullibody
Devonside
Bridge of Allan
Dunblane
Doune
Deanston
Thornhill
Callander (Calasraid)
Kilmahog
Port of Menteith
Blair Drummond
Kinbuck
Ashfield
Greenloaning
Blackford
Braco
Gleneagles
Auchterarder
Muirton
Aberuthven
Dunning
Kinkell Bridge
Muthill
Crieff
Gilmerton
Fowlis Wester
Madderty
Trinity Gask
Clathy
Findo Gask
Clathymore
Monzie
Hosh
Glenturret
Comrie
The Ross
Dalginross
St Fillans
Loch Earn
Lochearnhead
Ardvorich
Dalveich
Glen Lednock
Invergeldie
Loch Turret
Glen Artney
Dalchruin
Langside
Glen Eagles
Ochil Hills
Sheriffmuir
Glen Devon
Auchterarder
Sidlaw Hills
Burrelton
Kinrossie
Collace
Newmiln
Balholmie
Cargill
Wolfhill
Redstone
St Martin's

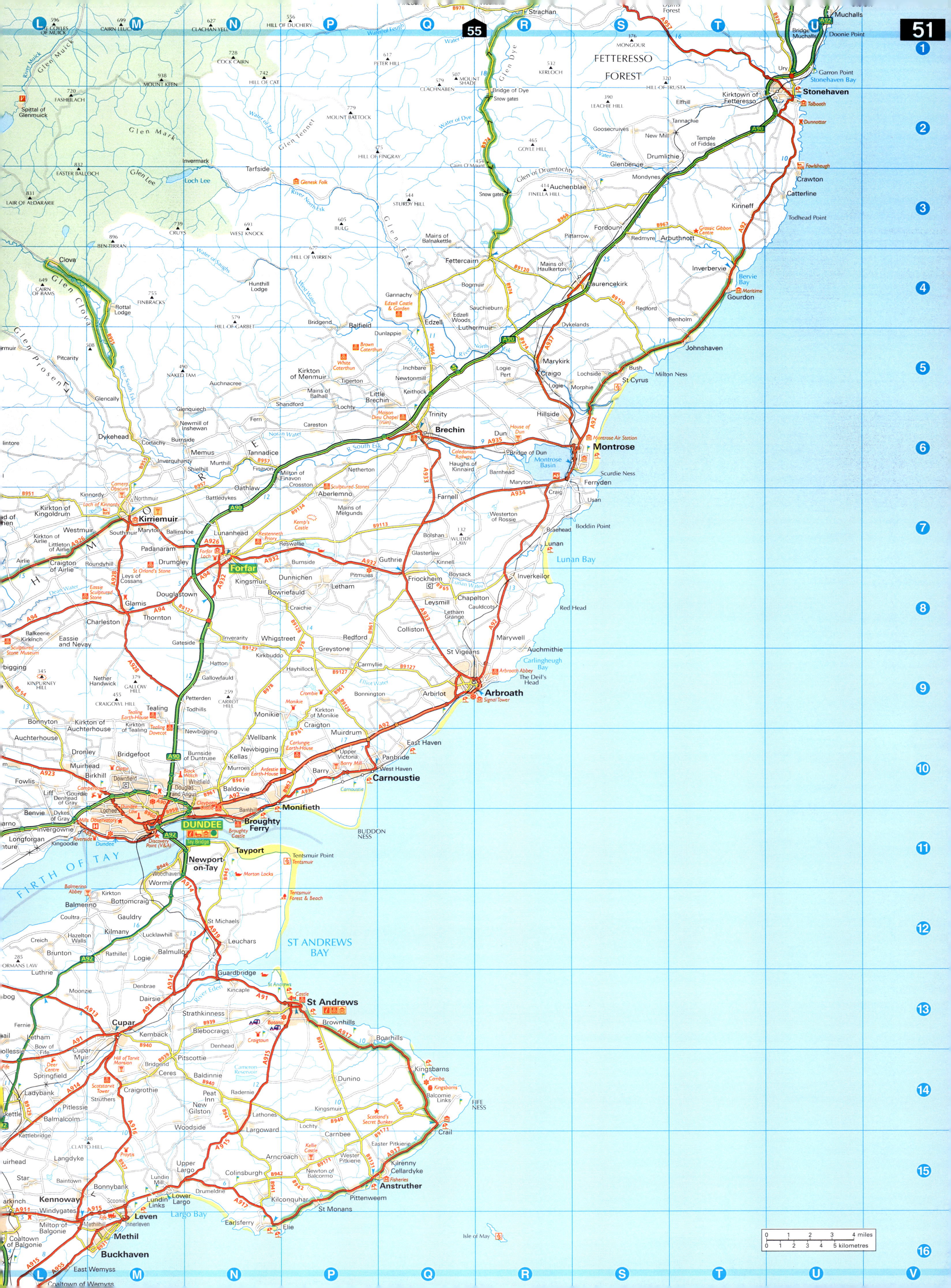
55
FETTERESSO
FOREST
Stonehaven
Stonehaven Bay
Garron Point
Doonie Point
Muchalls
Kirktown of Fetteresso
Strachan
Bridge of Dye
Glen Dye
Water of Feugh
Water of Dye
Glen Mark
Glen Lee
Glen Tennet
Glen Muick
Loch Lee
Tarfside
Invermark
River North Esk
Glen Esk
Glen Clova
Clova
Glen Prosen
River South Esk
Drumlithie
Glenbervie
Auchenblae
Fordoun
Arbuthnott
Catterline
Crawton
Kinneff
Todhead Point
Inverbervie
Bervie Bay
Gourdon
Johnshaven
Laurencekirk
Fettercairn
Edzell
Luthermuir
Marykirk
St Cyrus
Milton Ness
Brechin
Montrose
Montrose Basin
Ferryden
Scurdie Ness
Usan
Boddin Point
Lunan Bay
Lunan
Inverkeilor
Red Head
Auchmithie
Carlingheugh Bay
The Deil's Head
Arbroath
St Vigeans
Friockheim
Letham
Forfar
Kirriemuir
Glamis
Dundee
Broughty Ferry
Monifieth
Carnoustie
Buddon Ness
East Haven
Tayport
Newport-on-Tay
Tentsmuir Point
FIRTH OF TAY
ST ANDREWS BAY
Leuchars
Guardbridge
St Andrews
Boarhills
Kingsbarns
Fife Ness
Crail
Anstruther
Pittenweem
St Monans
Elie
Earlsferry
Largo Bay
Leven
Methil
Buckhaven
Kennoway
Cupar
Isle of May
A90
A92
A94
A93
A914
A915
A917
A91
0 1 2 3 4 miles
0 1 2 3 4 5 kilometres

Aultgrishin
Loch Ewe
Poolewe
North Erradale
Big Sand
Strath
Smithstown
Gairloch
Loch Gairloch
Longa Island
Port Henderson
Badachro
Opinan
South Erradale
Red Point
Charlestown
Talladale
Loch Maree
Wester Ross
Letterewe Forest
Kinlochewe
Incheril
Kinlochewe Forest
Fisherfield Forest
Loch na Sealga
Dundonnell Forest
Croftown
Auchindrean
Snow gates
Loch Torridon
Fearnmore
Lower Diabaig
Inveralligin
Alligin Shuas
Upper Loch Torridon
Torridon
Annat
Shieldaig
BEINN EIGHE
Glen Torridon
Glen Docherty
Achnasheen
Loch a' Chroisg
Glen Carron
Craig
Achnashellach
Balnacra
Coulags
Strathcarron
Achintee
Lochcarron
Kishorn
Loch Kishorn
Applecross
Applecross Bay
Milltown
Camusteel
Camusterrach
Culduie
Toscaig
Aird Dhubh
Kenmore
Arrina
Fearnbeg
Cuaig
Callakille
Lonbain
Glenshieldaig
Forest
Loch Damph
Loch Lundie
Loch Coultrie
Pass of the Cattle
Bealach na Bà
Rassal Ashwood
Slumbay
Attadale
Strome
Stromeferry
Ardnarff
Achmore
Plockton
Duirinish
Drumbuie
Port-an-Eorna
Badicaul
Balmacara
Reraig
Auchtertyre
Nostie
Conchra
Kyle of Lochalsh
(Caol Loch Aillse)
Skye Bridge
Kyleakin
Loch Alsh
Ardelve
Dornie
Eilean Donan
Bundalloch
Carndu
Killilan
Camas Luinie
Glen Elchaig
Falls of Glomach
Keppoch
Letterfearn
Loch Duich
Invershiel
Inverinate
Morvich
Shiel Bridge
Ratagan
Mam Ratagan
FIVE SISTERS
Kintail
Glen Shiel
Glen Affric
Affric Lodge
Cluanie Inn
Cluanie Lodge
Loch Cluanie
Glenquoich Forest
Glen Garry
Loch Quoich
Glen Kingie
Loch Arkaig
Glen Dessarry
Glen Pean
Murlaggan
Caonich
Ardechive
RAASAY
SOUND OF RAASAY
INNER SOUND
Rona
Eilean Tigh
Eilean Fladday
Torran
Arnish
Brochel
Oskaig
Inverarish
Clachan
Eyre Point
Suisnish Point
SCALPAY
Longay
Pabay
CROWLIN ISLANDS
Eilean Mòr
Eilean Meadhonach
Broadford
Broadford Bay
Corry
Waterloo
Lower Breakish
Breakish
Harrapool
Skulamus
Torrin
Kylerhea
Glenelg
Glenelg Bay
Bernera
Galltair
Eilanreach
Moyle
Glen Beag
Balvraid
Sandaig Islands
Loch Eishort
Isleornsay
Ornsay
Duisdalemore
Drumfearn
Heaste
Tokavaig
Tarskavaig
Tarskavaig Bay
Achnacloich
Teangue
Knock
Knock Bay
Ferrindonald
Kilmore
Kilbeg
Armadale
Armadale Castle
Ardvasar
Calligarry
Aird
Ard Thurinish
Point of Sleat
Strathaird Point
Glasnakille
Elgol
Kirkibost
SOUND OF SLEAT
Rubha Buidhe
Rubha Ard Slisneach
Loch Hourn
Arnisdale
Corran
Glen Arnisdale
Kinloch Hourn
Inverguseran
Glen Guseran
Airor
Sandaig
Inverie
Inverie Bay
KNOYDART
Knoydart
Loch Nevis
Kylesmorar
Tarbet
Swordland
Loch Morar
Mallaig
Mallaigvaig
Courteachan
Glasnacardoch Bay
Beoraidbeg
Morar
Bracora
Bracorina
Glenancross
0 1 2 3 4 miles
0 1 2 3 4 5 kilometres

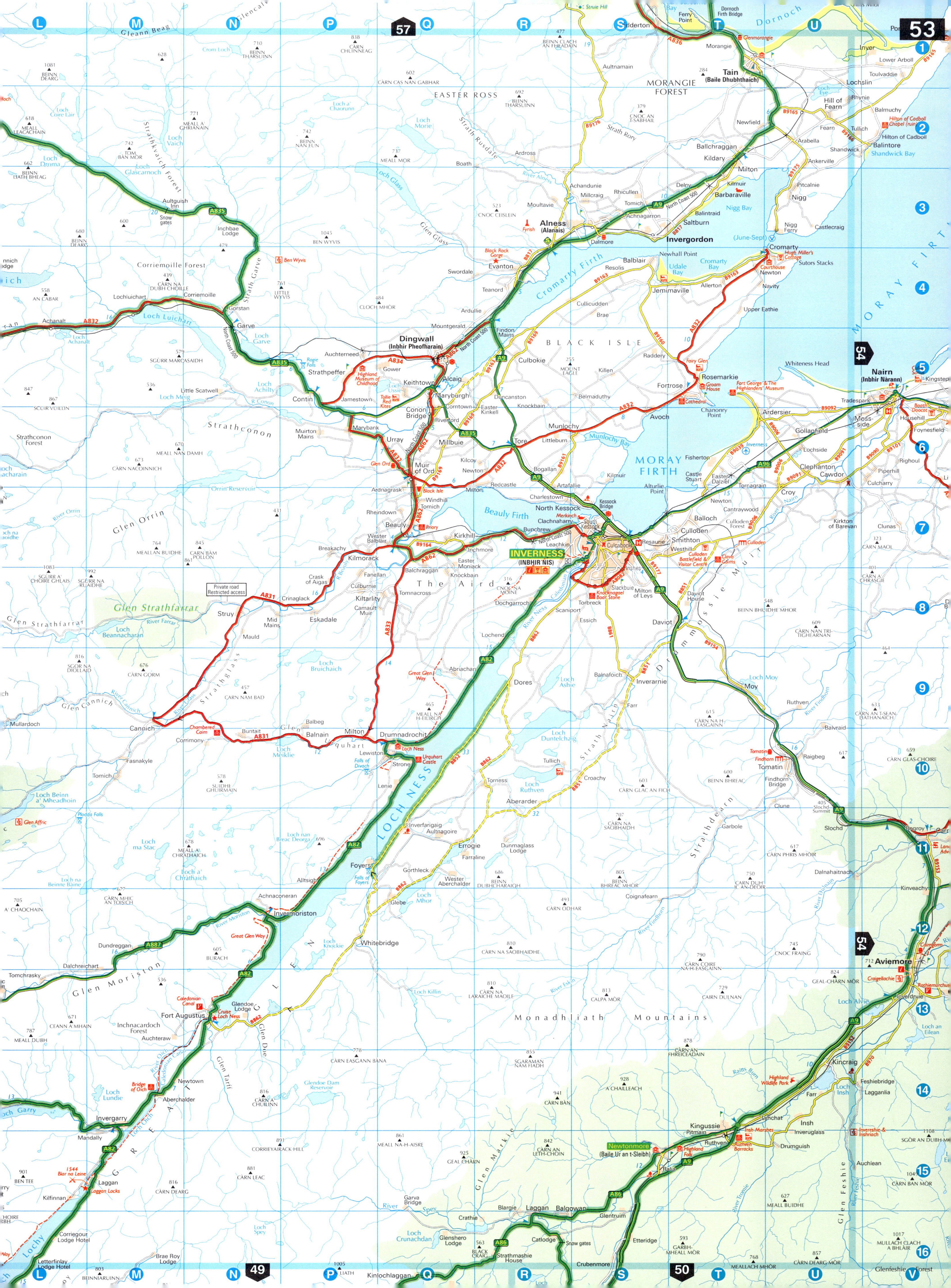
57
54
49
50
Dornoch Firth Bridge
Dornoch
Tain
(Baile Dhubhthaich)
MORANGIE FOREST
EASTER ROSS
Invergordon
Alness
(Alanais)
Cromarty
Cromarty Firth
BLACK ISLE
Dingwall
(Inbhir Pheofharain)
Strathpeffer
Contin
Garve
Loch Luichart
Loch Glascarnoch
Aultguish Inn
Corriemoillie Forest
Strathconon
Glen Orrin
Glen Strathfarrar
Glen Cannich
Cannich
Muir of Ord
Beauly
Beauly Firth
INVERNESS
(INBHIR NIS)
Culloden
Nairn
(Inbhir Narann)
MORAY FIRTH
Fortrose
Rosemarkie
Drumnadrochit
Urquhart Castle
LOCH NESS
Foyers
Dores
Invermoriston
Glen Moriston
Fort Augustus
Whitebridge
Strath Nairn
Monadhliath Mountains
Tomatin
Moy
Carrbridge
Aviemore
Kincraig
Kingussie
Newtonmore
(Baile Ur an t-Sleibh)
Laggan
Invergarry
Loch Lochy
Strath Dearn
Glen Feshie
Glen Markie
A9
A82
A835
A832
A862
A831
A887
A86
A96
North Coast 500

58
53
50
Lossiemouth
Elgin
Burghead
Burghead Bay
Hopeman
Duffus
Cummington
Findhorn
Kinloss
Forres
Nairn
(Inbhir Narann)
Auldearn
Cawdor
Croy
Ardersier
Culbin Forest
Dyke
Brodie
Rafford
Dallas
Alves
Kellas
Longmorn
Fogwatt
Rothes
Craigellachie
Aberlour
Charlestown of Aberlour
Dufftown
Archiestown
Knockando
Carron
Marypark
Glenlivet
Tomnavoulin
Tomintoul
Grantown-on-Spey
Cromdale
Advie
Ballindalloch
Bridge of Avon
Dava
Dava Moor
Lochindorb
Ferness
Carrbridge
Boat of Garten
Nethy Bridge
Dulnain Bridge
Aviemore
Coylumbridge
Kincraig
Feshiebridge
Insh
Kingussie
Glenmore Forest Park
Glenmore Lodge
CAIRNGORMS
CAIRNGORM NATIONAL PARK
CAIRNGORM MOUNTAINS
Cairn Gorm
Ben Macdhui
Braeriach
Cairn Toul
Ben Avon
Beinn a' Bhuird
Lochnagar
Braemar
Crathie
Balmoral
Ballater
Bridge of Gairn
Cambus o' May
Logie Coldstone
Strathdon
Corgarff
Cock Bridge
Glenkindie
Ladder Hills
Buckie
Portgordon
Spey Bay
Fochabers
Mosstodloch
Garmouth
Kingston on Spey
Urquhart
Lhanbryde
Keith
Maggieknockater
Drummuir
Cabrach
Findochty
Portessie
Rathven
Clochan
MORAY FIRTH
Cromarty
Nigg
Balintore
Shandwick
Portmahomack
Inver
Fearn
Tain
Whiteness Head
Findhorn Bay
Glen of Rothes
STRATH SPEY
Glen Livet
Glen Avon
Glen Feshie
Glen Derry
Lairig Ghru
Loch Insh
Loch Morlich
Loch Garten
Loch Kinord
Spey Bay
Gordon Castle
Balvenie Castle
Corgarff Castle
Balmoral Castle
Cawdor
Slochd
Tomatin
Duthil
Skye of Curr
Kirkton of Mortlach
Auchindoun Castle
Glenfiddich
Strathisla
Speyside Way
Lecht Ski Area
Cairngorm Ski Area
Highland Wildlife Park
Landmark Forest Adventure Park
Strathspey Railway
Keith & Dufftown Railway
A96
A95
A939
A940
A941
A9
A93
A97
A944
A920
B9102
B9008

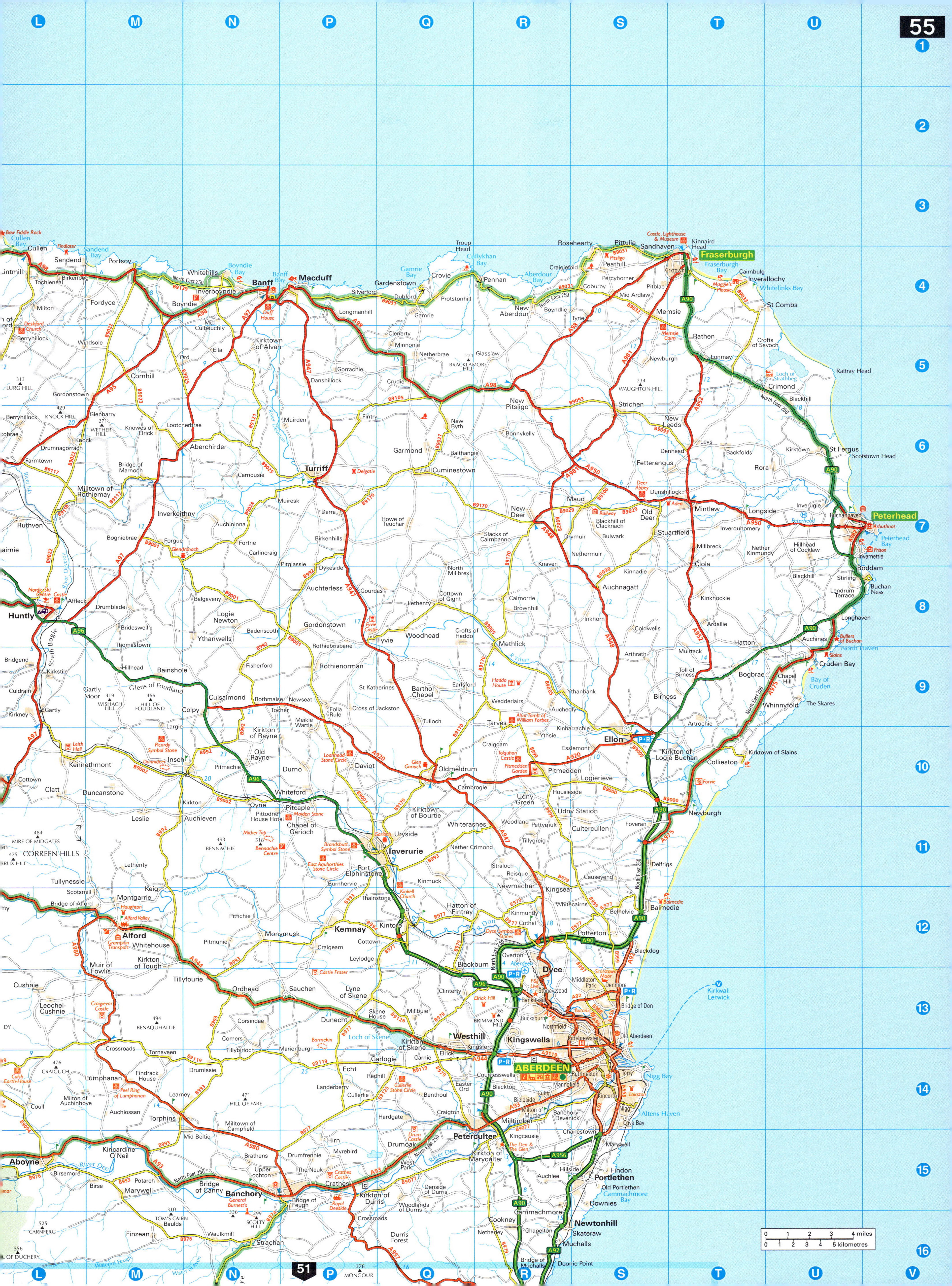
Fraserburgh
Peterhead
ABERDEEN
Cullen
Sandend
Portsoy
Banff
Macduff
Whitehills
Gardenstown
Crovie
Pennan
Troup Head
Rosehearty
Pittulie
Sandhaven
Kinnaird Head
Inverallochy
Cairnbulg
St Combs
Rattray Head
Crimond
St Fergus
Scotstown Head
Boddam
Buchan Ness
Longhaven
Cruden Bay
Bay of Cruden
The Skares
Whinnyfold
Collieston
Newburgh
Balmedie
Blackdog
Bridge of Don
Old Aberdeen
Nigg Bay
Altens Haven
Cove Bay
Portlethen
Findon
Newtonhill
Muchalls
Cammachmore Bay
Kirkwall
Lerwick
Huntly
Turriff
Fyvie
Methlick
Ellon
Oldmeldrum
Inverurie
Kintore
Kemnay
Monymusk
Alford
Aboyne
Banchory
Peterculter
Westhill
Kingswells
Dyce
Cults
Maud
Mintlaw
Old Deer
Stuartfield
New Deer
New Pitsligo
Strichen
New Aberdour
Memsie
Rathen
Auchnagatt
Hatton
Tarves
Pitmedden
Udny Green
Newmachar
Blackburn
Potterton
Muir of Fowlis
Tillyfourie
Insch
Kennethmont
Rhynie
Aberchirder
Cornhill
Fordyce
Auchterless
Cuminestown
Rothienorman
Whiterashes
Kingseat
Skene
Echt
Drumoak
Crathes
Strachan
Torphins
Lumphanan
Kincardine O'Neil
Stonehaven
Auchleven
Oyne
Chapel of Garioch
Daviot
Premnay
River Dee
River Don
River Deveron
River Ythan
Loch of Skene
Loch of Strathbeg
Bennachie
North East 250
A90
A96
A98
A947
A93
A944
A920
A950
A952
A97
A980
A981

Western Isles
0 5 10 miles
0 5 10 kilometres
OUTER HEBRIDES
ISLE OF LEWIS
HARRIS
RUBHA RHOBHANAIS (BUTT OF LEWIS)
Steòrnabhagh (Stornoway)
Tolastadh bho Thuath
Broad Bay
Chicken Head
Tiumpan Head
Cellar Head
Tolsta Head
PARK
THE MINCH
The Little Minch
Sound of Harris
An Tairbeart (Tarbert)
An t-Òb (Leverburgh)
Ròghadal (Rodel)
UIBHIST A TUATH (NORTH UIST)
Loch nam Madadh (Lochmaddy)
BEINN NA FAOGHLA (BENBECULA)
UIBHIST A DEAS (SOUTH UIST)
Loch Baghasdail (Lochboisdale)
BARRAIGH (BARRA)
Bàgh a' Chaisteil (Castlebay)
VATERSAY
MINGULAY
Berneray
SEA OF THE HEBRIDES
ISLE OF SKYE
Dunvegan
Uig
CANNA
Mallaig
Oban
Ullapool
59
CAPE WRATH
Kearvaig Bay
Sandwood Bay
Kinlochbervie
Rhiconich
HANDA ISLAND
Scourie
North-west Sutherland
Eddrachillis Bay
Kylestrome
Kylesku
Point of Stoer
Old Man of Stoer
Stoer
Clashnessie
Drumbeg
Glen Leirg
Lochinver
Assynt - Coigach
Inchnadamph
Loch Assynt
SUILVEN
CANISP
QUINAG
BEN MORE COIGACH
Enard Bay
Achiltibuie
SUMMER ISLES
COIGACH
Knockan
Elphin
Ledmore
Cromalt Hills
Strath Canaird
Isle Martin
Ullapool
Loch Broom
Little Loch Broom
Gruinard Bay
GRUINARD ISLAND
Laide
Aultbea
Dundonnell
ISLE OF EWE
Loch Ewe
Melvaig
Leckmelm
Inverlael Forest
North Coast 500
A835
A837
A894
A838
A832
52
A B C D E F G H J K
1 2 3 4 5 6 7 8 9 13 14 15 16
a b c d e f g
0 1 2 3 4 miles
0 1 2 3 4 5 kilometres

L
M
N
P
Q
R
S
T
U
1
2
3
4
5
6
7
8
9
10
12
13
14
15
16
Faraid Head
Balnakeil Bay
Balnakeil
Balnakeil Craft Village
Sango Bay
Durness
Smoo
Keoldale
Sangomore
Loch Airigh na Beinne
Sangobeg
Ceannabeinne
Loch Meadaidh
Kyle of Durness
Eilean Hoan
Whiten Head
Loch Eriboll
Portnancon
Laid
A838
North Coast 500
Strath Beag
Loch Hope
Strathmore River
Strath More
Dun Dornaigil Broch
Glen Golly
Kinloch
Loch Merkland
Loch Fiag
Glen Fiag
Overscaig
Loch Shin
Duchally
Glen Muic
Glen Cassley
Strath Oykel
Oykel Bridge
Rosehall
A837
Doune
Altass
Glen Einig
Strathcarron
Croick
Amat Forest
Glencalvie Forest
Kyle of Tongue
Tongue
Rabbit Islands
Talmine
Melness
Midtown
Strathan
Skerray
Achtoty
Torrisdale
Scullomie
Coldbackie
Tongue Bay
Eilean Nan Ròn
Neave or Coomb Island
Torrisdale Bay
Farr Bay
Farr
Farr Point
Bettyhill
Invernaver
Borgie
Achina
Strathnaver
Kirtomy Point
Kirtomy
Ardmore Point
Armadale
Armadale Bay
Swordly
A836
Skelpick
Strath Naver
B871
Syre
B873
Loch Naver
Altnaharra
Loch Loyal
Loch Loyal Lodge
Loch Craggie
Kinloch
Loch an Dherue
Strath Vagastie
Crask Inn
A836
Strath Tirry
Shinness
Achnairn
Colaboll
Sallachy
Lairg
Ferrycroft
Tomich
Torrobull
A839
Achany
Linsidemore
B864
Falls of Shin
Inveran
Invershin
Culrain
1650 Carbisdale
Kyle of Sutherland
Lower Gledfield
Ardgay
Kincardine
Ardchronie
Bonar Bridge
Migdale
Loch Migdale
A949
Spinningdale
Dornoch Firth
Struie Hill
Edderton
Ardmore
Meikle Ferry
Cambuscurrie Bay
Ferry Point
Whiteface
Clashmore
Cuthill
Dornoch Firth Bridge
Morangie
Glenmorangie
Loch Choire Forest
Ben Armine Forest
Borrobol Forest
Strath Skinsdale
Strath Brora
Loch Brora
Balnacoil
Dalreavoch
Pittentrail
Rogart
A839
Torboll
Loch Buidhe
Sleasdairidh
Achvaich
Rearquhar
Astle
Evelix
Birichin
Badninish
Cambusavie
Loch Fleet
Littleferry
Skelbo
Skelbo Street
Fourpenny
Embo
Embo Street
Pitgrudy
Royal Dornoch
Dornoch
Historylinks
Camore
A9
Dornoch Point
Golspie
Dunrobin Castle
Carn Liath
Backies
Rhives
Doll
Brora
Clynelish
Dalchalm
Strathy Point
Strathy Bay
Strathy
Strathy Inn
Brawl
Baligill
Melvich
Melvich Bay
Portskerra
Bighouse
River Strathy
Reay
Sandside Bay
Upper Dounreay
Isauld
Achvarasdal
Upper Bighouse
Strath Halladale
A897
Dalhalvaig
Trantlemore
Trantlebeg
Forsinard
Forsinard Flows
Loch an Ruathair
Kinbrace
B871
Badanloch
Loch Badanloch
Loch nan Clàr
Loch Rimsdale
Strath Free
Learable Hill Cairns, Stone Row & Stone Circles
Kildonan Lodge
Kildonan
Strath of Kildonan
Torrish
River Helmsdale
West Helmsdale
Gartymore
Portgower
Glen Loth
Lothmore
Lothbeg
KNOCKFIN HEIGHTS
Tarbat Ness
Wilkhaven
Portmahomack
Innis Mhor
Tarbat Discovery Centre
Inver
Rockfield
58
53
BEN HOPE
BEN LOYAL
BEN KLIBRECK
BEN HEE
BEN HORN
BEN DOULA
BEN GRIAM BEG
BEN GRIAM MOR
BEINN DONUILL
BEN LUNDIE

PENTLAND FIRTH
DUNNET HEAD
Dunnet Bay
Stromness
Thurso
Thurso Bay
Scrabster
Holborn Head
Brims Ness
Crosskirk
Forss
Reay
Sandside Bay
Strathy Point
Strathy Bay
Strathy
Melvich
Melvich Bay
Portskerra
Bighouse
Upper Bighouse
Armadale Bay
Brawl
Strathy Inn
Balinill
Achvarasdal
Shebster
Westfield
Geise
Loch Calder
Halkirk
Georgemas Junction Station
Spittal
Mybster
Westerdale
Castletown
Dunnet
Murkle
Olrig House
Weydale
Hilliclay
Sordale
Knockdee
Loch Scarmclate
Gillock
Watten
Loch Watten
Bilbster
Wick
Wick Bay
Staxigoe
Papigoe
Noss Head
Sinclair's Bay
Keiss
Reiss
Ackergill
Castle Sinclair Girnigoe
Lyth
Bower
Mey
Gills Bay
John o' Groats
DUNCANSBY HEAD
Canisbay
Freswick
Freswick Bay
Skirza
Skirza Head
Ness Head
Auckengill
Nybster
Brough Head
Slickly
Kirk
Halcro
Killimster
Winless
Haster
Milton
Newton
Old Wick
South Head
Castle of Old Wick
Loch Hempriggs
Tannach
Thrumster
Sarclet
Ulbster
Whaligoe
Whaligoe Steps
Bruan
Loch of Yarrows
HILL OF YARROWS
Roster
Hill o'Many Stanes
Mid Clyth
Clyth Ness
Occumster
Halberry Head
Lybster
Lybster Bay
Swiney
Upper Lybster
Forse
Inver
Latheron
Latheronwheel
Janetstown
Smerral
Landhallow
Dunbeath
Dunbeath Bay
Laidhay Croft
Knockally
Ramscraigs
Borgue
Newport
Langwell House
Berriedale
Badbea Historic Village
Ord of Caithness
Navidale
Helmsdale
West Helmsdale
East Helmsdale
Gartymore
Portgower
Lothmore
Lothbeg
Brora
Dalchalm
Doll
Backies
Golspie
Dunrobin Castle
Littleferry
Skelbo Street
Fourpenny
Embo
Embo Street
Dornoch
Royal Dornoch
Dornoch Point
Dornoch Firth
Inver
Portmahomack
Tarbat Ness
Wilkhaven
Rockfield
Tarbat Discovery Centre
Kinbrace
Forsinard
Forsinard Flows
Trantlebeg
Trantlemore
Dalhalvaig
Strath Halladale
Halladale River
KNOCKFIN HEIGHTS
Strath of Kildonan
Kildonan Lodge
Kildonan
River Helmsdale
Torrish
Strath Free
Dalnawillan Lodge
Glutt Lodge
Altnabreac Station
Scotscalder Station
Harpsdale
Broubster
Shurrery
Shurrery Lodge
Loch Shurrery
Dorrery
Olgrinmore
Langwell Forest
Braemore
MORVEN
SCARABEN
MAIDEN PAP
BEN ALISKY
Houstry
Achavanich
Loch Stemster
STEMSTER HILL
Loch Rangag
Loch More
Loch Ruard
Loch Sand
Loch Calium
Loch Tuim Ghlais
Loch Scye
Loch na Seilge
Loch Druim a' Chliabhain
Loch an Ruathair
Loch Arichlinie
Loch Brora
Loch Croacach
BEN GRIAM BEG
BEN GRIAM MOR
BEINN RUADH
BEINN RATHA
Loch Toftingall
Badlipster
BALLHARN HILL
Grey Cairns of Camster
Cairn o'Get
Clan Gunn Heritage Centre
A9
A99
A836
A882
A897
B871
B874
B876
Orkney Islands
KIRKWALL
Stromness
HOY
Scapa Flow
St Margaret's Hope
SOUTH RONALDSAY
SHAPINSAY
STRONSAY
SANDAY
WESTRAY
PAPA WESTRAY
NORTH RONALDSAY
ROUSAY
EDAY
EGILSAY
WYRE
Westray Firth
The North Sound
Sanday Sound
Stronsay Firth
Pentland Firth
Hoy Sound
Hoy and West Mainland
Burray
Lyness
Longhope
Melsetter
Burwick
ISLAND OF STROMA
Pentland Skerries
Some island ferry services are seasonal, day & weather dependent
10 miles
10 kilometres

56
Skye
0 5 10 miles
0 5 10 kilometres
SOUND OF SHIANT
SHIANT ISLANDS
An Tairbeart (Tarbert)
Aird Asaig (Ardhasig)
Reinigeadal (Rhenigidale)
Caolas Scalpaigh (Kyles Scalpay)
Sgalpaigh (Scalpay)
SCALPAY
Greosabhagh (Grosebay)
Scadabhagh (Scadabay)
Rubha Bhocaig
Loch nam Madadh (Lochmaddy)
Duntulm
Kilmaluag
Skye Museum of Island Life
Flodigarry
Staffin
Uig (Uige)
Loch Snizort
Trotternish
Kilt Rock
Rubha nam Brathairean
DUNVEGAN HEAD
Dunvegan
Edinbane
Portree
ISLE OF SKYE
SOUND OF RAASAY
RAASAY
RONA
INNER SOUND
Bracadale
Struan
Loch Harport
Carbost
Drynoch
Sligachan
Glen Varragill
The Braes
Peinchorran
SCALPAY
The Cuillin Hills
Cuillin Hills
Broadford
Kyle of Lochalsh (Caol Loch Aillse)
Skye Bridge
Kyleakin
Plockton
Loch Carron
Lochcarron
Stromeferry
Dornie
Eilean Donan
Shiel Bridge
Glenelg
Elgol
Loch Scavaig
SOAY
CUILLIN SOUND
SOUND OF SLEAT
Armadale
Point of Sleat
Isleornsay
KNOYDART
Inverie
Mallaig (Malaig)
CANNA
RÙM
Kinloch
The Small Isles
Sound of Canna
Sound of Rùm
All vehicles must have the relevant island permit prior to travel to The Small Isles. Services are seasonal, day & weather dependent.
52
48
A87
A850
A855
A863
A851
A890
A830
Shetland Islands
0 5 10 miles
0 5 10 kilometres
UNST
Haroldswick
Norwick
Baltasound
Uyeasound
FETLAR
YELL
Mid Yell
Ulsta
Burravoe
MAINLAND
Hillswick
Brae
Voe
St Magnus Bay
PAPA STOUR
Walls
LERWICK
Scalloway
BRESSAY
Isle of Noss
Sandwick
Sumburgh Head
Sumburgh Roost
OUT SKERRIES
WHALSAY
Some island ferry services are seasonal, day & weather dependent
FOULA
FAIR ISLE
Kirkwall Aberdeen

IRISH SEA
BELFAST
LONDONDERRY
DERRY
Donegal Bay
An Clochán Liath
Dunglow / Dungloe

Ireland

CELTIC SEA
Toll-free motorway
Toll motorway and plaza
Motorway junctions with and without number
Restricted motorway junctions
Motorway service area
National primary route (Republic of Ireland)
National secondary route (Republic of Ireland)
Regional route (Republic of Ireland)
Distance in kilometres between symbols (Republic of Ireland)
Primary route (Northern Ireland)
A road (Northern Ireland)
B road (Northern Ireland)
Distance in miles between symbols (Northern Ireland)
Minor road
Road tunnel, with toll
Road under construction
Airport
International boundary
Vehicle ferry
Fast vehicle ferry or catamaran
Gaeltacht (Irish language area)
National Park
For key to touring information see page I
To reflect the distances shown on road signs, distances are shown in miles in Northern Ireland and kilometres in the Republic of Ireland.
16 kilometres = 10 miles

Index to place names

This index lists places appearing in the main map section of the atlas in alphabetical order. The reference following each name gives the atlas page number and grid reference of the square in which the place appears. The map shows counties, unitary authorities and administrative areas, together with a list of the abbreviated name forms used in the index. In addition airports are indexed in blue *italic* and National Parks in green *italic*.

Scotland

Abers Aberdeenshire
Ag & B Argyll and Bute
Angus Angus
Border Scottish Borders
C Aber City of Aberdeen
C Dund City of Dundee
C Edin City of Edinburgh
C Glas City of Glasgow
Clacks Clackmannanshire (1)
D & G Dumfries & Galloway
E Ayrs East Ayrshire
E Duns East Dunbartonshire (2)
E Loth East Lothian
E Rens East Renfrewshire (3)
Falk Falkirk
Fife Fife
Highld Highland
Inver Inverclyde (4)
Mdloth Midlothian (5)
Moray Moray
N Ayrs North Ayrshire
N Lans North Lanarkshire (6)
Ork Orkney Islands
P & K Perth & Kinross
Rens Renfrewshire (7)
S Ayrs South Ayrshire
S Lans South Lanarkshire
Shet Shetland Islands
Stirlg Stirling
W Duns West Dunbartonshire (8)
W Isls Western Isles (Na h-Eileanan an Iar)
W Loth West Lothian

Wales

Blae G Blaenau Gwent (9)
Brdgnd Bridgend (10)
Caerph Caerphilly (11)
Cardif Cardiff
Carmth Carmarthenshire
Cerdgn Ceredigion
Conwy Conwy
Denbgs Denbighshire
Flints Flintshire
Gwynd Gwynedd
IoA Isle of Anglesey
Mons Monmouthshire
Myr Td Merthyr Tydfil (12)
Neath Neath Port Talbot (13)
Newpt Newport (14)
Pembks Pembrokeshire
Powys Powys
Rhondd Rhondda Cynon Taf (15)
Swans Swansea
Torfn Torfaen (16)
V Glam Vale of Glamorgan (17)
Wrexhm Wrexham

Channel Islands & Isle of Man

Guern Guernsey
Jersey Jersey
IoM Isle of Man

England

BaNES Bath & N E Somerset (18)
Barns Barnsley (19)
BCP Bournemouth, Christchurch and Poole (20)
Bed Bedford
Birm Birmingham
Bl w D Blackburn with Darwen (21)
Bolton Bolton (22)
Bpool Blackpool
Br & H Brighton & Hove (23)
Br For Bracknell Forest (24)
Bristl City of Bristol
Bucks Buckinghamshire
Bury Bury (25)
C Beds Central Bedfordshire
C Brad City of Bradford
C Derb City of Derby
C KuH City of Kingston upon Hull
C Leic City of Leicester
C Nott City of Nottingham
C Pete City of Peterborough
C Plym City of Plymouth
C Port City of Portsmouth
C Sotn City of Southampton
C Stke City of Stoke-on-Trent
C York City of York
Calder Calderdale (26)
Cambs Cambridgeshire
Ches E Cheshire East
Ches W Cheshire West and Chester
Cnwll Cornwall
Covtry Coventry
Cumb Cumberland
Darltn Darlington (27)
Derbys Derbyshire
Devon Devon
Donc Doncaster (28)
Dorset Dorset
Dudley Dudley (29)
Dur Durham
E R Yk East Riding of Yorkshire
E Susx East Sussex
Essex Essex
Gatesd Gateshead (30)
Gloucs Gloucestershire
Gt Lon Greater London
Halton Halton (31)
Hants Hampshire
Hartpl Hartlepool (32)
Herefs Herefordshire
Herts Hertfordshire
IoS Isles of Scilly
IoW Isle of Wight
Kent Kent
Kirk Kirklees (33)
Knows Knowsley (34)
Lancs Lancashire
Leeds Leeds
Leics Leicestershire
Lincs Lincolnshire
Lpool Liverpool
Luton Luton
M Keyn Milton Keynes
Manch Manchester
Medway Medway
Middsb Middlesbrough
N Linc North Lincolnshire
N Nthn North Northamptonshire
N Som North Somerset
N Tyne North Tyneside (35)
N u Ty Newcastle upon Tyne
N York North Yorkshire
NE Lin North East Lincolnshire
Norfk Norfolk
Notts Nottinghamshire
Nthumb Northumberland
Oldham Oldham (36)
Oxon Oxfordshire
R & Cl Redcar & Cleveland
Readg Reading
Rochd Rochdale (37)
Rothm Rotherham (38)
Rutlnd Rutland
S Glos South Gloucestershire (39)
S on T Stockton-on-Tees (40)
S Tyne South Tyneside (41)
Salfd Salford (42)
Sandw Sandwell (43)
Sefton Sefton (44)
Sheff Sheffield
Shrops Shropshire
Slough Slough (45)
Solhll Solihull (46)
Somset Somerset
St Hel St Helens (47)
Staffs Staffordshire
Sthend Southend-on-Sea
Stockp Stockport (48)
Suffk Suffolk
Sundld Sunderland
Surrey Surrey
Swindn Swindon
Tamesd Tameside (49)
Thurr Thurrock (50)
Torbay Torbay
Traffd Trafford (51)
W & F Westmorland & Furness
W & M Windsor & Maidenhead (52)
W Berk West Berkshire
W Nthn West Northamptonshire
W Susx West Sussex
Wakefd Wakefield (53)
Warrtn Warrington (54)
Warwks Warwickshire
Wigan Wigan (55)
Wilts Wiltshire
Wirral Wirral (56)
Wokham Wokingham (57)
Wolves Wolverhampton (58)
Worcs Worcestershire
Wrekin Telford & Wrekin (59)
Wsall Walsall (60)

A

Abbas Combe Somset 7 N7
Abberley Worcs 22 H14
Abberley Common Worcs 22 H14
Abberton Essex 19 M10
Abberton Worcs 15 R1
Abbess Roding Essex 18 F11
Abbeydale Sheff 31 U11
Abbey Dore Herefs 14 H5
Abbey Green Staffs 31 P14
Abbey Hulton C Stke 31 N16
Abbey St Bathans Border 46 K6
Abbeystead Lancs 35 P14
Abbeytown Cumb 39 T10
Abbey Village Lancs 30 J4
Abbey Wood Gt Lon 10 F2
Abbotrule Border 46 H14
Abbots Bickington Devon 4 H8
Abbots Bromley Staffs 23 M5
Abbotsbury Dorset 7 L13
Abbots Deuglie P & K 50 H14
Abbotsham Devon 4 J6
Abbotskerswell Devon 3 Q5
Abbots Langley Herts 17 N10
Abbots Leigh N Som 14 K14
Abbotsley Cambs 25 Q16
Abbots Morton Worcs 23 M16
Abbots Ripton Cambs 25 Q12
Abbot's Salford Warwks 15 S2
Abbots Worthy Hants 8 J6
Abbotts Ann Hants 8 F4
Abbott Street Dorset 7 S11
Abdon Shrops 22 E11
Aberaeron Cerdgn 20 C10
Aberaman Rhondd 14 B10
Aberangell Gwynd 20 H2
Aberarder Highld 53 R10
Aberargie P & K 50 J13
Aberarth Cerdgn 20 C10
Aberavon Neath 13 S12
Abercanaid Myr Td 14 C9
Abercarn Caerph 14 E11
Abercastle Pembks 12 D4
Abercegir Powys 20 H3
Aberchalder Highld 53 M14
Aberchirder Abers 55 M6
Abercorn W Loth 45 N4
Abercraf Powys 13 T8
Abercregan Neath 13 T10
Abercwmboi Rhondd 14 C10
Abercych Pembks 12 K3
Abercynon Rhondd 14 C11
Aberdalgie P & K 50 H12
Aberdare Rhondd 14 B10
Aberdaron Gwynd 28 B14
Aberdeen C Aber 55 S14
Aberdeen Airport C Aber 55 R13
Aberdour Fife 45 Q3
Aberdulais Neath 13 S10
Aberdyfi Gwynd 20 E4
Aberedw Powys 21 L12
Abereiddy Pembks 12 C5
Abererch Gwynd 28 E12
Aberfan Myr Td 14 C10
Aberfeldy P & K 50 D8
Aberffraw IoA 28 D7
Aberford Leeds 32 C1
Aberfoyle Stirlg 49 U16
Abergavenny Mons 14 F8
Abergele Conwy 29 M5
Abergorlech Carmth 13 P4
Abergwesyn Powys 20 H11
Abergwili Carmth 13 M7
Abergwynfi Neath 13 U11
Abergwyngregyn Gwynd 28 H6
Abergynolwyn Gwynd 20 F3
Aberkenfig Brdgnd 13 U13
Aberlady E Loth 46 F3
Aberlemno Angus 51 P7
Aberllefenni Gwynd 20 G2
Aberllynfi Powys 14 E4
Aberlour, Charlestown of Moray 54 G8
Abermule Powys 21 N5
Abernant Carmth 13 L6
Abernant Rhondd 14 B9
Abernethy P & K 50 J13
Abernyte P & K 50 K11
Aberporth Cerdgn 12 K2
Abersoch Gwynd 28 C14
Abersychan Torfn 14 F9
Aberthin V Glam 14 B14
Abertillery Blae G 14 E9
Abertridwr Caerph 14 D12
Abertridwr Powys 29 P15
Aberuthven P & K 50 F13
Aberystwyth Cerdgn 20 D7
Abingdon-on-Thames Oxon 16 E10
Abinger Common Surrey 9 S4
Abinger Hammer Surrey 9 S4
Abington S Lans 45 L13
Abington W Nthn 24 H15
Abington Pigotts Cambs 17 R3
Abingworth W Susx 9 S9
Ab Kettleby Leics 24 G5
Ablington Gloucs 15 T9
Abney Derbys 31 S11
Aboyne Abers 55 L15
Abhainn Suidhe W Isls 56 c3
Abram Wigan 30 J7
Abriachan Highld 53 Q9
Abridge Essex 18 E14
Abronhill N Lans 44 J4
Abson S Glos 15 M14
Abthorpe W Nthn 16 G2
Aby Lincs 33 S11
Acaster Malbis C York 37 L16
Acaster Selby N York 32 E1
Accrington Lancs 31 L3
Acha Ag & B 42 e2
Achahoish Ag & B 42 K4
Achalader P & K 50 H8
Achaleven Ag & B 49 L10
Acha Mor W Isls 56 e2
Achanalt Highld 53 L4
Achandunie Highld 53 S3
Achany Highld 57 P13
Acharacle Highld 48 G5
Acharn Highld 48 G7
Acharn P & K 50 C8
Achavanich Highld 58 F7
Achduart Highld 56 G13
Achfary Highld 56 K7
Achgarve Highld 56 D15
A'Chill Highld 59 c14
Achiltibuie Highld 56 F12
Achina Highld 57 R4
Achinhoan Ag & B 42 K14
Achintee Highld 52 G8
Achintraid Highld 52 E8
Achlyness Highld 56 K5
Achmelvich Highld 56 G10
Achmore Highld 52 E9
Achmore W Isls 56 e2
Achnacarnin Highld 56 G8
Achnacarry Highld 49 P1
Achnacloich Highld 59 g14
Achnaconeran Highld 53 N12
Achnacroish Ag & B 48 K9
Achnadrish Ag & B 48 D7
Achnafauld P & K 50 E10
Achnagarron Highld 53 S3
Achnaha Highld 48 D4
Achnahaird Highld 56 F11
Achnahannet Highld 54 C10
Achnairn Highld 57 P11
Achnalea Highld 48 K6
Achnamara Ag & B 42 K2
Achnasheen Highld 52 K5
Achnashellach Highld 52 G7
Achnastank Moray 54 H9
Achosnich Highld 48 D5
Achranich Highld 48 H8
Achreamie Highld 58 D3
Achriabhach Highld 49 P4
Achriesgill Highld 56 K5
Achtoty Highld 57 Q3
Achurch N Nthn 25 M11
Achvaich Highld 57 R15
Achvarasdal Highld 58 C3
Ackergill Highld 58 H5
Acklam Middsb 36 J4
Acklam N York 37 N13
Ackleton Shrops 22 H9
Acklington Nthumb 41 P2
Ackton Wakefd 32 C4
Ackworth Moor Top Wakefd 32 C5
Acle Norfk 27 T7
Acock's Green Birm 23 N11
Acol Kent 11 T4
Acomb C York 36 K15
Acomb Nthumb 40 K7
Aconbury Herefs 14 J4
Acton Ches E 30 J15
Acton Gt Lon 17 Q13
Acton Staffs 22 J2
Acton Suffk 19 L6
Acton Wrexhm 30 E15
Acton Beauchamp Herefs 15 M2
Acton Bridge Ches W 30 J12
Acton Burnell Shrops 22 E8
Acton Green Herefs 15 M2
Acton Round Shrops 22 F9
Acton Scott Shrops 21 S5
Acton Trussell Staffs 22 K6
Acton Turville S Glos 15 P13
Adbaston Staffs 22 H4
Adber Dorset 7 L7
Adbolton Notts 24 F2
Adderbury Oxon 16 E4
Adderley Shrops 22 G2
Addiewell W Loth 45 M6
Addingham C Brad 36 C15
Addington Bucks 16 H5
Addington Gt Lon 10 E4
Addington Kent 10 J5
Addiscombe Gt Lon 10 D4
Addlestone Surrey 17 N16
Addlethorpe Lincs 33 U13
Adeyfield Herts 17 N9
Adfa Powys 21 L4
Adforton Herefs 21 R9
Adisham Kent 11 S6
Adlestrop Gloucs 16 A6
Adlingfleet E R Yk 32 J4
Adlington Lancs 30 J5
Admaston Staffs 23 M5
Admaston Wrekin 22 F7
Adpar Cerdgn 12 K3
Adsborough Somset 6 G6
Adscombe Somset 6 E4
Adstock Bucks 16 H5
Adstone W Nthn 16 F2
Adswood Stockp 31 N10
Adversane W Susx 9 S8
Advie Highld 54 E9
Adwick le Street Donc 32 E6
Adwick upon Dearne Donc 32 D7
Ae D & G 39 R4
Ae Bridgend D & G 39 R4
Affleck Abers 55 M8
Affpuddle Dorset 7 P12
Affric Lodge Highld 52 K11
Afon-wen Flints 29 Q6
Afton IoW 8 F14
Agglethorpe N York 36 C9
Aigburth Lpool 30 F10
Aike E R Yk 37 S16
Aiketgate W & F 40 D11
Aikton Cumb 39 V10
Ailsworth C Pete 25 N9
Ainderby Quernhow N York 36 G10
Ainderby Steeple N York 36 G8
Aingers Green Essex 19 P10
Ainsdale Sefton 30 E6
Ainstable W & F 40 D11
Ainsworth Bury 31 L6
Ainthorpe N York 37 M5
Aintree Sefton 30 F8
Ainville W Loth 45 P6
Aird Ag & B 48 H16
Aird D & G 38 C8
Aird Highld 59 g15
Aird W Isls 56 f2
Àird a' Mhulaidh W Isls 56 d3
Aird Asaig W Isls 56 d4
Aird Dhubh Highld 52 C8
Airdeny Ag & B 49 M11
Airdrie N Lans 44 J6
Airdriehill N Lans 44 J6
Airds of Kells D & G 39 L7
Àird Uig W Isls 56 c2
Airidh a bhruaich W Isls 56 e3
Airieland D & G 39 M9
Airlie Angus 51 L7
Airmyn E R Yk 32 G3
Airntully P & K 50 H10
Airor Highld 52 C14
Airth Falk 45 L2
Airton N York 35 U13
Aisby Lincs 25 L2
Aisby Lincs 32 J9
Aish Devon 3 N6
Aish Devon 3 Q6
Aisholt Somset 6 F5
Aiskew N York 36 F9
Aislaby N York 37 N9
Aislaby N York 37 P5
Aislaby S on T 36 H5
Aisthorpe Lincs 33 L11
Aith Shet 59 p5
Akeld Nthumb 47 N12
Akeley Bucks 16 H4
Albaston Cnwll 2 J4
Alberbury Shrops 21 Q1
Albourne W Susx 10 C12
Albrighton Shrops 22 D6
Albrighton Shrops 22 J8
Alburgh Norfk 27 R11
Albury Herts 18 D9
Albury Surrey 9 R4
Albury Heath Surrey 9 R4
Alcaig Highld 53 Q5
Alcaston Shrops 21 S6
Alcester Warwks 23 N16
Alciston E Susx 10 G14
Alcombe Somset 5 S3
Alconbury Cambs 25 P13
Alconbury Weald Cambs 25 P13
Alconbury Weston Cambs 25 P12
Aldborough N York 36 H12
Aldborough Norfk 27 Q3
Aldbourne Wilts 16 B14
Aldbrough E R Yk 33 Q1
Aldbrough St John N York 36 E5
Aldbury Herts 17 M8
Aldcliffe Lancs 35 N13
Aldclune P & K 50 E5
Aldeburgh Suffk 19 U4
Aldeby Norfk 27 T10
Aldenham Herts 17 P10
Alderbury Wilts 8 D7
Alderford Norfk 27 P6
Alderholt Dorset 8 C10
Alderley Gloucs 15 N11
Alderley Edge Ches E 31 M11
Aldermans Green Covtry 23 R11
Aldermaston W Berk 16 F16
Alderminster Warwks 15 V2
Aldershot Hants 9 P3
Alderton Gloucs 15 R4
Alderton Suffk 19 S6
Alderton W Nthn 16 H2
Alderton Wilts 15 P13
Aldfield N York 36 F12
Aldford Ches W 30 F14
Aldgate Rutlnd 25 L8
Aldham Essex 19 L9
Aldham Suffk 19 N6
Aldingbourne W Susx 9 Q11
Aldingham W & F 34 K11
Aldington Kent 11 Q9
Aldington Worcs 15 S3
Aldington Corner Kent 11 P9
Aldivalloch Moray 54 J10
Aldochlay Ag & B 44 C2
Aldreth Cambs 26 D13
Aldridge Wsall 23 M9
Aldringham Suffk 19 T3
Aldsworth Gloucs 15 T8
Aldunie Moray 54 J10
Aldwark Derbys 31 T15
Aldwark N York 36 J13
Aldwick W Susx 9 P12
Aldwincle N Nthn 25 L12
Aldworth W Berk 16 F13
Alexandria W Duns 44 D3
Aley Somset 6 E4
Alfington Devon 6 D11
Alfold Surrey 9 R6
Alfold Crossways Surrey 9 R6
Alford Abers 55 M12
Alford Lincs 33 T12
Alford Somset 7 L5
Alfreton Derbys 32 C15
Alfrick Worcs 15 N1
Alfrick Pound Worcs 15 N1
Alfriston E Susx 10 G14
Algarkirk Lincs 25 Q3
Alhampton Somset 7 M5
Alkborough N Linc 32 K4
Alkham Kent 11 S8
Alkmonton Derbys 23 P2
Allaleigh Devon 3 P7
Allanaquoich Abers 54 E16
Allanbank N Lans 44 K7
Allanton Border 47 M8
Allanton N Lans 44 K7
Allanton S Lans 44 J8
Allaston Gloucs 15 L9
Allbrook Hants 8 H8
All Cannings Wilts 15 S16
Allendale Nthumb 40 J9
Allen End Warwks 23 P9
Allenheads Nthumb 40 J11
Allen's Green Herts 18 D10
Allensmore Herefs 14 J4
Allenton C Derb 23 S3
Aller Devon 5 P6
Aller Somset 6 H6
Allerby Cumb 39 S12
Allercombe Devon 6 C12
Allerford Somset 5 R3
Allerston N York 37 Q10
Allerthorpe E R Yk 37 N15
Allerton C Brad 31 R2
Allerton Highld 53 T4
Allerton Lpool 30 F10
Allerton Bywater Leeds 32 C3
Allerton Mauleverer N York 36 H14
Allesley Covtry 23 R12
Allestree C Derb 23 R2
Allexton Leics 24 J9
Allgreave Ches E 31 P13
Allhallows Medway 11 L2
Alligin Shuas Highld 52 E5
Allington Dorset 6 J12
Allington Lincs 24 J2
Allington Wilts 8 D5
Allington Wilts 15 Q14
Allington Wilts 15 S16
Allithwaite W & F 35 L11
Alloa Clacks 45 L1
Allonby Cumb 39 S11
Alloway S Ayrs 43 T14
Allowenshay Somset 6 H8
All Stretton Shrops 21 S4
Alltchaorunn Highld 49 P7
Alltsigh Highld 53 P11
Alltwalis Carmth 13 M5
Alltwen Neath 13 R9
Alltyblaca Cerdgn 20 D13
Almeley Herefs 21 Q12
Almington Staffs 22 G3
Almondbank P & K 50 G11
Almondbury Kirk 31 S5
Almondsbury S Glos 15 L13
Alne N York 36 J12
Alness Highld 53 S3
Alnham Nthumb 47 N15
Alnmouth Nthumb 47 S15
Alnwick Nthumb 47 R14
Alperton Gt Lon 17 Q13
Alphamstone Essex 18 K7
Alpheton Suffk 18 K5
Alphington Devon 5 R12
Alport Derbys 31 T13
Alpraham Ches E 30 J14
Alresford Essex 19 N10
Alrewas Staffs 23 P6
Alsager Ches E 31 M15
Alsop en le Dale Derbys 31 S15
Alston Devon 6 G10
Alston W & F 40 G11
Alstone Gloucs 15 R5
Alstonefield Staffs 31 R15
Alston Sutton Somset 6 J2
Alswear Devon 5 N7
Altandhu Highld 56 F11
Altarnun Cnwll 4 F14
Altass Highld 57 N14
Altcreich Ag & B 48 G9
Altgaltraig Ag & B 43 P4
Althorne Essex 19 L13
Althorpe N Linc 32 J6
Altnabreac Station Highld 58 D6
Altnaharra Highld 57 P8
Altofts Wakefd 32 C4
Alton Derbys 32 B13
Alton Hants 9 M5
Alton Staffs 23 M2
Alton Barnes Wilts 15 T16
Alton Pancras Dorset 7 N10
Alton Priors Wilts 15 T16
Altrincham Traffd 31 L10
Altskeith Hotel Stirlg 49 T15
Alva Clacks 50 E16
Alvanley Ches W 30 G12
Alvaston C Derb 23 S3
Alvechurch Worcs 23 M13
Alvecote Warwks 23 Q8
Alvediston Wilts 7 R7
Alveley Shrops 22 H11
Alverdiscott Devon 4 K6
Alverstoke Hants 8 K12
Alverstone IoW 8 K14
Alverthorpe Wakefd 31 U4
Alverton Notts 24 H2
Alves Moray 54 F4
Alvescot Oxon 16 B9
Alveston S Glos 15 L12
Alveston Warwks 23 Q16
Alvingham Lincs 33 R9
Alvington Gloucs 15 L10
Alwalton C Pete 25 N9
Alweston Dorset 7 M8
Alwinton Nthumb 47 M16
Alwoodley Leeds 31 U1
Alyth P & K 50 K8
Am Bàgh a Tuath W Isls 56 b8
Ambergate Derbys 32 B16
Amberley Gloucs 15 P10
Amberley W Susx 9 R9
Amble Nthumb 41 Q1
Amblecote Dudley 22 K11
Ambler Thorn C Brad 31 R3
Ambleside W & F 35 L6
Ambleston Pembks 12 F6
Ambrosden Oxon 16 G7
Amcotts N Linc 32 J5
Amersham Bucks 17 L10
Amersham Common Bucks 17 M10
Amersham Old Town Bucks 17 L10
Amersham on the Hill Bucks 17 M10
Amesbury Wilts 8 D5
Amhuinnsuidhe W Isls 56 c3
Amington Staffs 23 Q8
Amisfield D & G 39 R5
Amlwch IoA 28 E3
Ammanford Carmth 13 Q8
Amotherby N York 37 N11
Ampfield Hants 8 G8
Ampleforth N York 36 K10
Ampney Crucis Gloucs 15 S10
Ampney St Mary Gloucs 15 T10
Ampney St Peter Gloucs 15 S10
Amport Hants 8 F4
Ampthill C Beds 17 N4
Ampton Suffk 26 K13
Amroth Pembks 12 H9
Amulree P & K 50 E10
Amwell Herts 17 P8
Anaheilt Highld 48 J5
Ancaster Lincs 25 L2
Ancells Farm Hants 9 N2
Ancroft Nthumb 47 P9
Ancrum Border 46 H13
Ancton W Susx 9 Q11
Anderby Lincs 33 U12
Andover Hants 8 G4
Andoversford Gloucs 15 S7
Andreas IoM 34 e2
Anerley Gt Lon 10 D3
Anfield Lpool 30 F9
Angarrack Cnwll 1 P11
Angelbank Shrops 22 E13
Angle Pembks 12 D9
Anglesey IoA 28 E5
Angmering W Susx 9 S11
Angram N York 36 K15
Ankerville Highld 53 U2
Ankle Hill Leics 24 H6
Anlaby E R Yk 33 M3
Anmer Norfk 26 H4
Anmore Hants 9 L10
Annan D & G 39 U7
Annat Highld 52 F6
Annathill N Lans 44 H5
Anna Valley Hants 8 F4
Annbank S Ayrs 44 D13
Annfield Plain Dur 41 N10
Anniesland C Glas 44 F5
Ansdell Lancs 30 E3
Ansford Somset 7 M5
Ansley Warwks 23 R10
Anslow Staffs 23 P5
Anslow Gate Staffs 23 P5
Anstey Herts 18 D8
Anstey Leics 24 E7
Anstruther Fife 51 Q15
Ansty W Susx 10 D11
Ansty Warwks 23 S11
Ansty Wilts 7 R6
An Tairbeart W Isls 56 d4
Anthorn Cumb 39 U9
Antingham Norfk 27 R3
An t-Ob W Isls 56 c4
Anton's Gowt Lincs 25 R1
Antony Cnwll 2 J7
Antrobus Ches W 30 K11
Anwick Lincs 33 N16
Anwoth D & G 38 K9
Aperfield Gt Lon 10 E5
Apethorpe N Nthn 25 M9
Apley Lincs 33 N12
Apperknowle Derbys 32 C11
Apperley Gloucs 15 P5
Appin Ag & B 49 L8
Appleby N Linc 33 L5
Appleby-in-Westmorland W & F 35 R3
Appleby Magna Leics 23 R7
Appleby Parva Leics 23 R7
Applecross Highld 52 C7
Appledore Devon 4 J6
Appledore Devon 6 D8
Appledore Kent 11 N10
Appleford Oxon 16 E11
Applegarth Town D & G 39 S4
Appleshaw Hants 8 F4
Appleton Halton 30 H10
Appleton Oxon 16 D10
Appleton Warrtn 30 J10
Appleton-le-Moors N York 37 N9
Appleton-le-Street N York 37 N11
Appleton Roebuck N York 36 K16
Appleton Thorn Warrtn 30 J10
Appleton Wiske N York 36 H6
Appletreehall Border 46 G14
Appletreewick N York 36 C13
Appley Somset 6 D7
Apse Heath IoW 8 J14
Apsley End C Beds 17 P5
Apuldram W Susx 9 N11
Arabella Highld 53 U2
Arbirlot Angus 51 Q9
Arborfield Wokham 16 J15
Arborfield Cross Wokham 16 J15
Arbourthorne Sheff 32 B10
Arbroath Angus 51 R9
Arbuthnott Abers 51 T3
Archddu Carmth 13 M10
Archdeacon Newton Darltn 36 F4
Archencarroch W Duns 44 D3
Archiestown Moray 54 G7
Arclid Ches E 31 M14
Ardallie Abers 55 T8
Ardanaiseig Hotel Ag & B 49 N12
Ardaneaskan Highld 52 E9
Ardarroch Highld 52 E8
Ardbeg Ag & B 42 E9
Ardbeg Ag & B 43 P6
Ardbeg Ag & B 43 Q3
Ardcharnich Highld 56 H15
Ardchiavaig Ag & B 48 C13
Ardchonnell Ag & B 49 L14
Ardchronie Highld 57 Q15
Ardchullarie More Stirlg 49 V13
Arddarroch Ag & B 43 R1
Arddleen Powys 29 S15
Ard Dorch Highld 59 g11
Ardechive Highld 49 P1
Ardeer N Ayrs 43 S10
Ardeley Herts 17 R5
Ardelve Highld 52 F10
Arden Ag & B 44 C3
Ardens Grafton Warwks 15 T1
Ardentallen Ag & B 48 J12
Ardentinny Ag & B 43 R2
Ardentraive Ag & B 43 P4
Ardeonaig Stirlg 50 B10
Ardersier Highld 53 T6
Ardessie Highld 56 G15
Ardfern Ag & B 48 J15
Ardfernal Ag & B 42 G5
Ardgartan Ag & B 49 R15
Ardgay Highld 57 P15
Ardgour Highld 49 M5
Ardgowan Inver 43 R5
Ardhallow Ag & B 43 Q4
Ardhasig W Isls 56 d4
Ardheslaig Highld 52 D5
Ardindrean Highld 56 H15
Ardingly W Susx 10 D10
Ardington Oxon 16 D12
Ardlamont Ag & B 43 N6
Ardleigh Essex 19 N8
Ardleigh Heath Essex 19 N8
Ardler P & K 50 K9
Ardley Oxon 16 F5
Ardlui Ag & B 49 R13
Ardlussa Ag & B 42 H2
Ardmair Highld 56 H14
Ardmaleish Ag & B 43 P5
Ardminish Ag & B 42 H9
Ardmolich Highld 48 H4
Ardmore Ag & B 43 T4
Ardmore Highld 57 R16
Ardnadam Ag & B 43 Q3
Ardnagrask Highld 53 Q6
Ardnarff Highld 52 F9
Ardnastang Highld 48 J6
Ardpatrick Ag & B 42 K7
Ardrishaig Ag & B 43 L2
Ardross Highld 53 R2
Ardrossan N Ayrs 43 R10
Ardslignish Highld 48 F6
Ardtalla Ag & B 42 F8
Ardtoe Highld 48 F4
Arduaine Ag & B 48 J14
Ardullie Highld 53 R4
Ardvasar Highld 52 B14
Ardvorlich P & K 50 A12
Ardvourlie W Isls 56 d3
Ardwell D & G 38 C11
Ardwick Manch 31 N8
Areley Kings Worcs 22 J13
Arevegaig Highld 48 G4
Arford Hants 9 N6
Argoed Caerph 14 E10
Aribruach W Isls 56 e3
Aridhglas Ag & B 48 B12
Arileod Ag & B 42 d2
Arinagour Ag & B 42 e2
Ariogan Ag & B 48 K11
Arisaig Highld 48 G1
Arisaig House Highld 48 G2
Arkendale N York 36 H13
Arkesden Essex 18 E8
Arkholme Lancs 35 P11
Arkleton D & G 40 B3
Arkley Gt Lon 17 Q11
Arksey Donc 32 E6
Arkwright Town Derbys 32 C12
Arle Gloucs 15 Q6
Arlecdon Cumb 34 G4
Arlesey C Beds 17 Q4
Arleston Wrekin 22 G7
Arley Ches E 30 K11
Arlingham Gloucs 15 M8
Arlington Devon 5 M4
Arlington E Susx 10 G14
Armadale Highld 52 B14
Armadale Highld 57 S3
Armadale W Loth 45 L5
Armathwaite W & F 40 D11
Arminghall Norfk 27 R8
Armitage Staffs 23 M6
Armley Leeds 31 T2
Armscote Warwks 16 A3
Armthorpe Donc 32 F7
Arnabost Ag & B 42 e2
Arncliffe N York 35 U11
Arncroach Fife 51 P15
Arndilly House Moray 54 H7
Arne Dorset 7 R13
Arnesby Leics 24 F10
Arngask P & K 50 J14
Arnisdale Highld 52 E13
Arnish Highld 59 g8
Arniston Mdloth 46 D6
Arnol W Isls 56 e1
Arnold E R Yk 33 N1
Arnold Notts 24 E1
Arnprior Stirlg 44 G1
Arnside W & F 35 M10
Aros Ag & B 48 F8
Arrad Foot W & F 34 K10
Arram E R Yk 37 S16
Arran N Ayrs 43 M11
Arrathorne N York 36 E8
Arreton IoW 8 J14
Arrina Highld 52 D5
Arrington Cambs 17 S2
Arrochar Ag & B 49 R15
Arrow Warwks 23 N16
Arscott Shrops 21 R2
Artafallie Highld 53 R6
Arthington Leeds 36 F16
Arthingworth W Nthn 24 H12
Arthrath Abers 55 S9
Artrochie Abers 55 T9
Arundel W Susx 9 R10
Asby Cumb 34 G3
Ascog Ag & B 43 Q6
Ascot W & M 17 L15
Ascott-under-Wychwood Oxon 16 B7
Asenby N York 36 H11
Asfordby Leics 24 G6
Asfordby Hill Leics 24 G6
Asgarby Lincs 25 N1
Ash Kent 10 H4
Ash Kent 11 T5
Ash Somset 6 J7
Ash Surrey 9 P3
Ashampstead W Berk 16 F14
Ashbocking Suffk 19 Q4

B

C

D

E

I

J

K

L

M

N

O

P

Q

R

S

U

V

W

Y

Z